Mahāsatipaṭṭhāna Sutta

The Great Discourse on the Establishing of Awareness

This is a revised edition of the text in Roman-script Pāli with translation into English for the use of participants in a meditation course on the Satipaṭṭhāna Sutta, *as taught by S. N. Goenka.*

A Scriptural Research Project of:
Vipassana Research Institute

Published by
Vipassana Research Publications
Onalaska, WA, U.S.A.

Vipassana Research Publications

an imprint of

Pariyatti Publishing

867 Larmon Road

Onalaska, WA 98570, U.S.A.

First printed as *Mahā Satipaṭṭhāna Suttanta,* 1985, by Vipassana Research Institute (VRI), Igatpuri, India

Reprinted by VRI as *Mahāsatipaṭṭhāna Suttaṃ,* 1993

First United States edition, 1996

Reprinted, 2005, 2010, 2016

ISBN: 978-0-9649484-0-2 (Print)

ISBN: 978-1-928706-84-7 (eBook)

Library of Congress Cataloging-in-Publication Data

Tipiṭaka. Suttapiṭaka. Dīghanikāya. Mahāsatipaṭṭhānasutta. English and Pāli.

Mahāsatipaṭṭhāna sutta : the great discourse on the establishing of awareness. — 1st U.S. ed.

p. cm.

"This is a revised edition of the text in Roman-script Pāli with translation into English for the use of participants in a meditation course on the Satipaṭṭhāna Sutta as taught by S.N. Goenka."

ISBN 0-09-649484-0 (pbk. : alk. paper)

I. Title

BQ1320.S2522E5 1996

294.3'823 — dc20 96-22631

CIP

Printed in China

Vedanānaṃ samudayaṃ ca atthaṅgamaṃ ca assādaṃ ca ādīnavaṃ ca nissaranaṃ ca yathābhūtaṃ viditvā anupādāvimutto, bhikkhave, tathāgato.

Dīgha-nikāya I. 36, *Brahmajāla Sutta*

Having experienced as they really are, the arising of sensations, their passing away, the relishing of them, the danger in them and the release from them, the Enlightened One, monks, is fully liberated, being free from all attachment.

Visayasūci

Contents

Note on the Pronunciation of Pāli

Pāli was a spoken language of northern India in the time of Gotama the Buddha. It was written in the Brahmī script in India in the time of Emperor Asoka and has been preserved in the scripts of the various countries where the language has been maintained. In Roman script the following set of diacritical marks are used to indicate the proper pronunciation.

The alphabet consists of forty-one characters: eight vowels and thirty-three consonants.

Vowels: a, ā, i, ī, u, ū, e, o

Consonants:

Velar:	k	kh	g	gh	n
Palatal:	c	ch	j	jh	ñ
Retroflex:	ṭ	ṭh	ḍ	ḍh	ṇ
Dental:	t	th	d	dh	n
Labial:	p	ph	b	bh	m
Miscellaneous:	y, r, l, v, s, h, ḷ, ṃ				

The vowels **a, i, u** are short; **ā, ī, ū** are long; **e** and **o** are pronounced long except before double consonants: *deva, mettā; loka, phoṭṭhabbā.*

a is pronounced like 'a' in 'about'; **ā** like 'a' in 'father';
i is pronounced like 'i' in 'mint'; **ī** like 'ee' in 'see';
u is pronounced like 'u' in 'put'; **ū** like 'oo' in 'pool'.

The consonant **c** is pronounced as in the 'ch' in 'church'. All the aspirated consonants are pronounced with an audible expulsion of breath following the normal unaspirated sound. Therefore **th** is not as in 'three' but more like the sound in 'Thailand', and **ph** is not as in 'photo' but rather is pronounced 'p' accompanied by an expulsion of breath.

The retroflex consonants, **ṭ, ṭh, ḍ, ḍh, ṇ** are pronounced with the tip of the tongue turned back, whereas in the dentals, **t, th, d, dh, n,** it touches the upper front teeth.

The palatal nasal, **ñ,** is the same as the Spanish 'ñ', as in señor. The velar nasal, **ṅ,** is pronounced like 'ng' in 'singer' but occurs only with the other consonants in its group: *ṅk, ṅkh, ṅg, ṅgh.* The pronunciation of **ṃ** is similar to **ṅ** but occurs most commonly as a terminal nasalization: *'evaṃ me sutaṃ'.* The Pāli **v** is a soft 'v' or 'w' and **ḷ**, produced with the tongue retroflexed, is almost a combined 'rl' sound.

Vedanā in the Practice of *Satipaṭṭhāna*

Vipassana Research Institute

The practice of the four-fold *satipaṭṭhāna*, the establishing of awareness, was highly praised by the Buddha in the suttas. Mentioning its importance in the *Mahāsatipaṭṭhāna Sutta*, the Buddha called it *ekāyano maggo*—the only way for the purification of beings, for overcoming sorrow, for extinguishing suffering, for walking on the path of truth and for realising *nibbāna* (liberation).[1]

In this sutta, the Buddha presented a practical method for developing self-knowledge by means of *kāyānupassanā* (observation of the body), *vedanānupassanā* (observation of sensations), *cittānupassanā* (observation of the mind), and *dhammānupassanā* (observation of the contents of the mind).[2]

To explore the truth about ourselves, we must examine what we are: body and mind. We must learn to observe these directly within ourselves. Accordingly, we must keep three points in mind: 1) The reality of the body may be imagined by contemplation, but to experience it directly one must work with *vedanā* (body sensations) arising within it. 2) Similarly, the actual experience of the mind is attained by working with the contents of the mind. Therefore, in the same way as body and sensations cannot be experienced separately, the mind cannot be observed apart from the contents of the mind.

3) Mind and matter are so closely inter-related that the contents of the mind always manifest themselves as sensations in the body. For this reason the Buddha said:

Vedanā-samosaraṇā sabbe dhammā.[3]

Everything that arises in the mind flows together with sensations.

Therefore, observation of sensations offers a means — indeed the only means — to examine the totality of our being, physical as well as mental.

Broadly speaking, the Buddha refers to five types of *vedanā:*

1. *Sukhā vedanā* — pleasant sensations
2. *Dukkhā vedanā* — unpleasant sensations
3. *Somanassa vedanā* — pleasant mental feeling
4. *Domanassa vedanā* — unpleasant mental feeling
5. *Adukkhamasukhā vedanā* — neither unpleasant nor pleasant sensations.

In all references to *vedanā* in the *Satipaṭṭhāna Sutta* the Buddha speaks of *sukhā vedanā, dukkhā vedanā,* i.e., the body sensations; or *adukkhamasukhā vedanā,* which in this context also clearly denotes neutral body sensations.

The strong emphasis is on body sensations because they work as a direct avenue for the attainment of fruition *(nibbāna)* by means of "strong dependence condition" *(upanissaya-paccayena paccayo),* i.e., the nearest dependent condition for our liberation. This fact is succinctly highlighted in the *Paṭṭhāna,* the seventh text of *Abhidhamma Piṭaka* under the *Pakatupanissaya,* where it is stated:

Kāyikaṃ sukhaṃ kāyikassa sukhassa, kāyikassa dukkhassa, phalasamāpattiyā upanissayapaccayena paccayo.

Kāyikaṃ dukkhaṃ kāyikassa sukhassa, kāyikassa dukkhassa, phalasamāpattiyā upanissayapaccayena paccayo.

> *Utu kāyikassa sukhassa, kāyikassa dukkhassa, phalasamāpattiyā upanissayapaccayena paccayo.*
>
> *Bhojanaṃ kāyikassa sukhassa, kāyikassa dukkhassa, phalasamāpattiyā upanissayapaccayena paccayo.*
>
> *Senāsanaṃ kāyikassa sukhassa, kāyikassa dukkhassa, phalasamāpattiyā upanissayapaccayena paccayo.*[4]
>
> Bodily pleasure is related to bodily pleasure, bodily pain, and attainment of fruition *(nibbāna)* by strong dependence condition.
>
> Bodily pain is related to bodily pleasure, bodily pain, and attainment of fruition by strong dependence condition.
>
> The season (or surrounding environment) is related to bodily pleasure, bodily pain, and attainment of fruition by strong dependence condition.
>
> Food is related to bodily pleasure, bodily pain, and attainment of fruition by strong dependence condition.
>
> Lying down and sitting (i.e., the mattress and cushions, or the position of lying, sitting, etc.) is related to bodily pleasure, bodily pain, and attainment of fruition by strong dependence condition.

From the above statement it is clear how important *vedanā,* is on the path of liberation. Pleasure and pain in the body, the surrounding environment *(utu),* the food we eat *(bhojanaṃ),* and the sleeping and sitting position, the mattress or cushions used, etc. *(senāsanaṃ)* are all responsible for ongoing body sensations of one type or another. When the sensations are experienced properly, as the Buddha explained in *Mahāsatipaṭṭhāna Sutta,* these become the nearest dependent condition for our liberation.

There are four dimensions to our nature: the body and its sensations, and the mind and its contents. These provide four avenues for the establishing of awareness in *satipaṭṭhāna.* In order that the observation be complete, we must experience every facet, which we can only do by means of *vedanā.* This exploration of truth will remove the delusions we have about ourselves.

In the same way, to come out of the delusion about the world outside, we must explore how the outside world interacts with our own mind-and-matter phenomenon, our own self. The outside world comes in contact with the individual only at the six sense doors: the eye, ear, nose, tongue, body and mind. Since all these sense doors are contained in the body, every contact of the outside world is at the body level.

The traditional spiritual teachers of India, before the Buddha, in his day and afterwards, expressed the view that craving causes suffering and that to remove suffering one must abstain from the objects of craving. This belief led to various practices of penance and extreme abstinence from external stimuli. In order to develop detachment, the Buddha took a different approach. Having learned to examine the depths of his own mind, he realized that between the external object and the mental reflex of craving is a missing link: *vedanā.* Whenever we encounter an object through the five physical senses or the mind, a sensation arises; and based on the sensation, *taṇhā* (craving) arises. If the sensation is pleasant we crave to prolong it, if it is unpleasant we crave to be rid of it. It is in the chain of Dependent Origination *(paṭiccasamuppāda)* that the Buddha expressed his profound discovery:

Saḷāyatana-paccayā phasso
Phassa-paccayā vedanā
Vedanā-paccayā taṇhā.[5]

Dependent on the six sense-spheres, contact arises.
Dependent on contact, sensation arises.
Dependent on sensation, craving arises.

The immediate cause for the arising of craving and, consequently, of suffering is not something outside of us but rather the sensations that occur within us.

Therefore, just as the understanding of *vedanā* is absolutely essential to understand the interaction between mind and matter within ourselves, the same understanding of *vedanā* is essential to understand the interaction of the outside world with the individual.

If this exploration of truth were to be attempted by contemplation or intellectualization, we could easily ignore the importance of *vedanā*. However, the crux of the Buddha's teaching is the necessity of understanding the truth not merely at the intellectual level, but by direct experience. For this reason *vedanā* is defined as follows:

> *Yā vedeti ti vedanā, sā vediyati lakkhaṇā, anubhavana-rasā...*[6]
>
> That which feels the object is *vedanā;* its characteristic is to feel, it is the essential taste of experience...

However, merely to feel the sensations within is not enough to remove our delusions. Instead, it is essential to understand the *ti-lakkhaṇā* (three characteristics) of all phenomena. We must directly experience *anicca* (impermanence), *dukkha* (suffering), and *anatta* (selflessness) within ourselves. Of these three the Buddha always stressed the importance of *anicca* because the realization of the other two will easily follow when we experience deeply the characteristic of impermanence. In the *Meghiya Sutta* of the *Udāna* he said:

> *Aniccasaññino hi, Meghiya, anattasaññā saṇṭhāti, anattasaññī asmimānasamugghātaṃ pāpuṇāti diṭṭheva dhamme nibbānaṃ.*[7]
>
> In one, Meghiya, who perceives impermanence, the perception of selflessness is established. One who perceives what is selfless wins the uprooting of the pride of egotism in this very life, and thus realizes *nibbāna*.

Therefore, in the practice of *satipaṭṭhāna,* the experience of *anicca,* arising and passing away, plays a crucial role. This experience of *anicca* as it manifests in the mind and body is also called *vipassanā.* The practice of Vipassana is the same as the practice of *satipaṭṭhāna.*

The *Mahāsatipaṭṭhāna Sutta* begins with the observation of the body. Here several different starting points are explained: observing respiration, giving attention to bodily movements, etc. It is from these points that we can progressively develop *vedanānupassanā, cittānupassanā* and *dhammānupassanā.* However, no matter from which point the journey starts, stages come which everyone must pass through on the way to the final goal. These are described in important sentences repeated not only at the end of each section of *kāyānupassanā* but also at the end of *vedanānupassanā, cittānupassanā* and each section of *dhammānupassanā.* They are:

1. *Samudaya-dhammānupassī vā viharati.*
2. *Vaya-dhammānupassī vā viharati.*
3. *Samudaya-vaya-dhammānupassī vā viharati.*[8]

1. One dwells observing the phenomenon of arising.
2. One dwells observing the phenomenon of passing away.
3. One dwells observing the phenomenon of arising and passing away.

These sentences reveal the essence of the practice of *satipaṭṭhāna.* Unless these three levels of *anicca* are experienced, we will not develop *paññā* (wisdom) — the equanimity based on the experience of impermanence — which leads to detachment and liberation. Therefore, in order to practise any of the four-fold *satipaṭṭhānā* we have to develop the constant thorough understanding of impermanence which in Pāli is known as *sampajañña.*

Sampajañña has been often misunderstood. In the colloquial language of the day it also had the meaning of "knowingly." For example, the Buddha has spoken of *sampajānamusā bhāsitā,*[9] and *sampajāna musāvāda*[10] which means "consciously, or knowingly, to speak falsely." This superficial meaning of the term is sufficient in an ordinary context. But whenever the Buddha speaks of *vipassanā*, of the practice leading to purification, to *nibbāna,* as here in this *sutta,* then *sampajañña* has a specific, technical significance.

To remain *sampajāno* (the adjective form of *sampajañña*), one must meditate on the impermanence of phenomena *(anicca-bodha),* objectively observing mind and matter without reaction. The understanding of *samudaya-vaya-dhammā* (the nature of arising and passing away) cannot be by contemplation, which is merely a process of thinking, or by imagination or even by believing; it must be performed with *paccanubhoti*[11] (direct experience), which is *yathābhūta-ñāṇa-dassana*[12] (experiential knowledge of the reality as it is). Here the observation of *vedanā* plays its vital role, because with *vedanā* a meditator very clearly and tangibly experiences *samudaya-vaya* (arising and passing away). *Sampajañña,* in fact, is directly perceiving the arising and passing away of *vedanā,* wherein all four facets of our being are included.

It is for this reason that the three essential qualities—to remain *ātāpī* (ardent), *sampajāno,* and *satimā* (aware)—are invariably repeated for each of the four *satipaṭṭhānas.* And as the Buddha explained, *sampajañña* is observing the arising and passing away of *vedanā.*[13] Hence the part played by *vedanā* in the practice of *satipaṭṭhāna* should not be ignored or this practice of *satipaṭṭhāna* will not be complete.

In the words of the Buddha:

> *Tisso imā, bhikkhave, vedanā. Katamā tisso? Sukhā vedanā, dukkhā vedanā, adukkhamasukhā vedanā. Imā kho, bhikkhave, tisso vedanā. Imāsaṃ kho, bhikkhave, tissannaṃ vedanānaṃ pariññāya cattāro satipaṭṭhānā bhāvetabbā.*[14]
>
> Meditators, there are three types of body sensations. What

> are the three? Pleasant sensations, unpleasant sensations and neutral sensations. Meditators, these are the three types of sensations. Practise, meditators, the four-fold satipaṭṭhānā for the complete understanding of these three sensations.

The practice of *satipaṭṭhāna,* which is the practice of Vipassana, is complete only when one directly experiences impermanence. Sensations provide the nexus where the entire mind and body are tangibly revealed as impermanent phenomena, leading to liberation.

References

1. *Dīgha-nikāya*: VRI.II.373; PTS.II.290
2. *Loc. cit.*
3. fr. *Mūlaka Sutta* in *Aṅguttara-nikāya,* VRI.III, *Dasakanipāta,* 58; PTS.V.107
4. *Paṭṭhāna,* Vol. I, *Kusalatika:* VRI.324
5. *Vinaya, Mahāvagga:* VRI.1; PTS.2
6. *Abhidhammattha-saṅgaho,* Hindi translation and commentary by Ven. Dr. U Rewata Dhamma, Varanaseya Sanskrit Vishva-vidyalaya, Varanasi, Vol. I p. 101. By using the term *anubhavanarasā* the commentator is pointing to the fact that the essence of experience itself is *vedanā,* the sensations on the body.
7. *Udāna:* VRI.31; PTS.37
8. *Dīgha-nikāya:* VRI.II.374-404; PTS II. 292-314
9. *Dīgha-nikāya:* VRI.III.62; PTS.III.45. *Aṅguttara-nikāya :* VRI.I, *Tikanipāta,* 28; PTS.I.128
10. *Vinaya, Pācittiya:* VRI.3; PTS.2
11. *Majjhima-nikāya:*VRI.I.455; PTS.I.295; *Saṃyutta-nikāya:* VRI. III.512, 823 ff., 839 ff.; PTS.V.217, 264ff., 286ff.
12. *Aṅguttara-nikāya:* VRI.II, *Pañcakanipāta,* 24, 168, *Sattakanipāta,* 65, VRI.III, *Aṭṭhakanipāta,* 81; PTS.III.19, 200; IV.99,336
13. *Saṃyutta-nikāya:* VRI.III.401; PTS.V.180
14. *Ibid.*: VRI.III.415; PTS.V.180

Note: Pāli references are from the *Chaṭṭha Saṅgāyana* edition of the *Tipiṭaka,* published by the Vipassana Research Institute (VRI), giving book and paragraph number, followed by the Pali Text Society (PTS) edition, giving book and page number.

Namo Tassa
Bhagavato Arahato
Sammāsambuddhassa

Mahāsatipaṭṭhāna Sutta

Evaṃ me sutaṃ.

Ekaṃ samayaṃ bhagavā kurūsu viharati kammāsadhammaṃ nāma kurūnaṃ nigamo. Tatra kho bhagavā bhikkhū āmantesi, 'Bhikkhavo'[1] ti. 'Bhaddante' ti te bhikkhū bhagavato paccassosuṃ. Bhagavā etadavoca:

1. Uddeso

Ekāyano ayaṃ, bhikkhave, maggo sattānaṃ visuddhiyā, sokaparidevānaṃ samatikkamāya, dukkhadomanassānaṃ atthaṅgamāya, ñāyassa adhigamāya, nibbānassa sacchikiriyāya, yadidaṃ cattāro satipaṭṭhānā.[2]

Katame cattāro? Idha, bhikkhave, bhikkhu kāye kāyānupassī viharati ātāpī sampajāno[3] satimā, vineyya loke abhijjhādomanassaṃ. Vedanāsu vedanānupassī viharati ātāpī sampajāno satimā, vineyya loke abhijjhādomanassaṃ. Citte cittānupassī viharati ātāpī sampajāno satimā, vineyya loke abhijjhādomanassaṃ. Dhammesu dhammānupassī viharati ātāpī sampajāno satimā, vineyya loke abhijjhādomanassaṃ.[4]

The Great Discourse on the Establishing of Awareness

Thus have I heard:

At one time the Enlightened One was staying among the Kurus at Kammāsadhamma, a market town of the Kuru people. There the Enlightened One addressed the monks thus: "Monks,"[1] and they replied, "Venerable Sir!" Then the Enlightened One spoke as follows:

1. Introduction

This is the one and only way, monks, for the purification of beings, for the overcoming of sorrow and lamentation, for the extinguishing of suffering and grief, for walking on the path of truth, for the realisation of *nibbāna:* that is to say, the fourfold establishing of awareness.[2]

Which four? Here, monks, a monk dwells ardent with awareness and constant thorough understanding of impermanence,[3] observing body in body, having removed craving and aversion towards the world [of mind and matter]; he dwells ardent with awareness and constant thorough understanding of impermanence, observing sensations in sensations, having removed craving and aversion towards the world [of mind and matter]; he dwells ardent with awareness and constant thorough understanding of impermanence, observing mind in mind, having removed craving and aversion towards the world [of mind and matter]; he dwells ardent with awareness and constant thorough understanding of impermanence, observing mental contents in mental contents, having removed craving and aversion towards the world [of mind and matter].[4]

2. Kāyānupassanā

A. Ānāpānapabbaṃ

Kathaṃ ca pana, bhikkhave, bhikkhu kāye kāyānupassī viharati?

Idha, bhikkhave, bhikkhu araññagato vā rukkhamūlagato vā suññāgāragato vā nisīdati pallaṅkaṃ ābhujitvā, ujuṃ kāyaṃ paṇidhāya, parimukhaṃ satiṃ upaṭṭhapetvā. So sato va assasati, sato va passasati. Dīghaṃ vā assasanto 'dīghaṃ assasāmī' ti pajānāti,[5] dīghaṃ vā passasanto 'dīghaṃ passasāmī' ti pajānāti. Rassaṃ vā assasanto 'rassaṃ assasāmī' ti pajānāti, rassaṃ vā passasanto 'rassaṃ passasāmī' ti pajānāti. 'Sabbakāyapaṭisaṃvedī assasissāmī' ti sikkhati, 'sabbakāyapaṭisaṃvedī passasissāmī' ti sikkhati. 'Passambhayaṃ kāyasaṅkhāraṃ assasissāmī' ti sikkhati, 'passambhayaṃ kāyasaṅkhāraṃ passasissāmī' ti sikkhati.

Seyyathāpi, bhikkhave dakkho bhamakāro vā bhamakārantevāsī vā dīghaṃ vā añchanto 'dīghaṃ añchāmī' ti pajānāti, rassaṃ vā añchanto 'rassaṃ añchāmī' ti pajānāti. Evameva kho, bhikkhave, bhikkhu dīghaṃ vā assasanto 'dīghaṃ assasāmī' ti pajānāti, dīghaṃ vā passasanto 'dīghaṃ passasāmī' ti pajānāti, rassaṃ vā assasanto 'rassaṃ assasāmī' ti pajānāti, rassaṃ vā passasanto 'rassaṃ passasāmī' ti pajānāti. 'Sabbakāyapaṭisaṃvedī assasissāmī' ti sikkhati, 'sabbakāyapaṭisaṃvedī passasissāmī' ti sikkhati, 'passambhayaṃ kāyasaṅkhāraṃ assasissāmī' ti sikkhati, 'passambhayaṃ kāyasaṅkhāraṃ passasissāmī' ti sikkhati.

2. The Observation of Body

A. Section on Respiration

And how, monks, does a monk dwell observing body in body?

Here a monk, having gone into the forest, or to the foot of a tree, or to an empty room, sits down cross-legged, keeps his body upright and fixes his awareness in the area around the mouth. With this awareness, he breathes in, with this awareness, he breathes out. Breathing in a deep breath, he understands properly:[5] "I am breathing in a deep breath." Breathing out a deep breath, he understands properly: "I am breathing out a deep breath." Breathing in a shallow breath he understands properly: "I am breathing in a shallow breath." Breathing out a shallow breath, he understands properly: "I am breathing out a shallow breath." In this way he trains himself: "Feeling the whole body, I shall breathe in." "Feeling the whole body, I shall breathe out," thus he trains himself. "With the bodily activities calmed, I shall breathe in," thus he trains himself. "With the bodily activities calmed, I shall breathe out," thus he trains himself.

Just as a skilful turner or a turner's apprentice, while making a long turn understands properly: "I am making a long turn," and while making a short turn, understands properly: "I am making a short turn," just so, the monk, breathing in a deep breath, understands properly: "I am breathing in a deep breath." Breathing out a deep breath, he understands properly: "I am breathing out a deep breath." Breathing in a shallow breath, he understands properly: "I am breathing in a shallow breath." Breathing out a shallow breath, he understands properly: "I am breathing out a shallow breath." In this way he trains himself: "Feeling the whole body, I shall breathe in." "Feeling the whole body, I shall breathe out," thus he trains himself. "With the bodily activities calmed, I shall breathe in," thus he trains himself. "With the bodily activities calmed, I shall breathe out," thus he trains himself.

Iti[6] ajjhattaṃ vā kāye kāyānupassī viharati, bahiddhā[7] vā kāye kāyānupassī viharati, ajjhattabahiddhā vā kāye kāyānupassī viharati, samudayadhammānupassī vā kāyasmiṃ viharati, vayadhammānupassī vā kāyasmiṃ viharati, samudayavaya-dhammānupassī vā kāyasmiṃ viharati, 'atthi kāyo'[8] ti vā panassa sati paccupaṭṭhitā hoti. Yāvadeva ñāṇamattāya paṭissatimattāya[9] anissito ca viharati, na ca kiñci loke upādiyati. Evaṃ pi kho, bhikkhave, bhikkhu kāye kāyānupassī viharati.

B. Iriyāpathapabbaṃ

Puna caparaṃ, bhikkhave, bhikkhu gacchanto vā 'gacchāmī' ti pajānāti, ṭhito vā 'ṭhitomhī' ti pajānāti, nisinno vā 'nisinnomhī' ti pajānāti, sayāno vā 'sayānomhī' ti pajānāti. Yathā yathā vā panassa kāyo paṇihito hoti, tathā tathā naṃ pajānāti.[10]

Iti ajjhattaṃ vā kāye kāyānupassī viharati, bahiddhā vā kāye kāyānupassī viharati, ajjhattabahiddhā vā kāye kāyānupassī viharati, samudayadhammānupassī vā kāyasmiṃ viharati, vayadhammānupassī vā kāyasmiṃ viharati, samudayavaya-dhammānupassī vā kāyasmiṃ viharati, 'atthi kāyo' ti vā panassa sati paccupaṭṭhitā hoti. Yāvadeva ñāṇamattāya paṭissatimattāya anissito ca viharati, na ca kiñci loke upādiyati. Evaṃ pi kho, bhikkhave, bhikkhu kāye kāyānupassī viharati.

Thus[6] he dwells observing body in body internally, or he dwells observing body in body externally, or he dwells observing body in body both internally and externally.[7] Thus he dwells observing the phenomenon of arising in the body, thus he dwells observing the phenomenon of passing away in the body, thus he dwells observing the phenomenon of arising and passing away in the body. Now his awareness is established: "This is body!"[8] Thus he develops his awareness to such an extent that there is mere understanding along with mere awareness.[9] In this way he dwells detached, without clinging towards anything in the world [of mind and matter]. This is how, monks, a monk dwells observing body in body.

B. Section on Postures

Again, monks, a monk while he is walking, understands properly: "I am walking"; while he is standing, he understands properly: "I am standing"; while he is sitting, he understands properly: "I am sitting"; while he is lying down, he understands properly: "I am lying down." In whichever position he disposes his body, he understands it properly.[10]

Thus he dwells observing body in body internally, or he dwells observing body in body externally, or he dwells observing body in body both internally and externally. Thus he dwells observing the phenomenon of arising in the body, thus he dwells observing the phenomenon of passing away in the body, thus he dwells observing the phenomenon of arising and passing away in the body. Now his awareness is established: "This is body!" Thus he develops his awareness to such an extent that there is mere understanding along with mere awareness. In this way he dwells detached, without clinging towards anything in the world [of mind and matter]. This is how, monks, a monk dwells observing body in body.

C. Sampajānapabbaṃ

Puna caparaṃ, bhikkhave, bhikkhu abhikkante paṭikkante sampajānakārī hoti,[11] ālokite vilokite sampajānakārī hoti, samiñjite pasārite sampajānakārī hoti, saṅghāṭipatta-cīvaradhāraṇe sampajānakārī hoti, asite pīte khāyite sāyite sampajānakārī hoti, uccārapassāvakamme sampajānakārī hoti, gate ṭhite nisinne sutte jāgarite bhāsite tuṇhībhāve sampajānakārī hoti.

Iti ajjhattaṃ vā kāye kāyānupassī viharati, bahiddhā vā kāye kāyānupassī viharati, ajjhattabahiddhā vā kāye kāyānupassī viharati, samudayadhammānupassī vā kāyasmiṃ viharati, vayadhammānupassī vā kāyasmiṃ viharati, samudayavaya-dhammānupassī vā kāyasmiṃ viharati, 'atthi kāyo' ti vā panassa sati paccupaṭṭhitā hoti. Yāvadeva ñāṇamattāya paṭissatimattāya anissito ca viharati, na ca kiñci loke upādiyati. Evaṃ pi kho, bhikkhave, bhikkhu kāye kāyānupassī viharati.

C. Section on Constant Thorough Understanding of Impermanence

Again, monks, a monk, while going forward or backward, he does so with constant thorough understanding of impermanence;[11] whether he is looking straight ahead or looking sideways, he does so with constant thorough understanding of impermanence; while he is bending or stretching, he does so with constant thorough understanding of impermanence; whether wearing his robes or carrying his bowl, he does so with constant thorough understanding of impermanence; whether he is eating, drinking, chewing or savouring, he does so with constant thorough understanding of impermanence; while attending to the calls of nature, he does so with constant thorough understanding of impermanence; whether he is walking, standing, sitting, sleeping or waking, speaking or in silence, he does so with constant thorough understanding of impermanence.

Thus he dwells observing body in body internally, or he dwells observing body in body externally, or he dwells observing body in body both internally and externally. Thus he dwells observing the phenomenon of arising in the body, thus he dwells observing the phenomenon of passing away in the body, thus he dwells observing the phenomenon of arising and passing away in the body. Now his awareness is established: "This is body!" Thus he develops his awareness to such an extent that there is mere understanding along with mere awareness. In this way he dwells detached, without clinging towards anything in the world [of mind and matter]. This is how, monks, a monk dwells observing body in body.

D. Paṭikūlamanasikārapabbaṃ

Puna caparaṃ, bhikkhave, bhikkhu imameva kāyaṃ, uddhaṃ pādatalā adho kesamatthakā, tacapariyantaṃ pūraṃ nānappakārassa asucino paccavekkhati: 'Atthi imasmiṃ kāye kesā lomā nakhā dantā taco maṃsaṃ nhāru aṭṭhi aṭṭhimiñjaṃ vakkaṃ hadayaṃ yakanaṃ kilomakaṃ pihakaṃ papphāsaṃ antaṃ antaguṇaṃ udariyaṃ karīsaṃ pittaṃ semhaṃ pubbo lohitaṃ sedo medo assu vasā kheḷo siṅghāṇikā lasikā muttaṃ' ti.

Seyyathāpi, bhikkhave, ubhatomukhā putoḷi pūrā nānāvihitassa dhaññassa, seyyathidaṃ sālīnaṃ vīhīnaṃ muggānaṃ māsānaṃ tilānaṃ taṇḍulānaṃ. Tamenaṃ cakkhumā puriso muñcitvā paccavekkheyya: 'Ime sālī ime vīhī, ime muggā, ime māsā, ime tilā, ime taṇḍulā' ti; evameva kho, bhikkhave, bhikkhu imameva kāyaṃ, uddhaṃ pādatalā adho kesamatthakā, tacapariyantaṃ pūraṃ nānappakārassa asucino paccavekkhati: 'Atthi imasmiṃ kāye kesā lomā nakhā dantā taco maṃsaṃ nhāru aṭṭhi aṭṭhimiñjaṃ vakkaṃ hadayaṃ yakanaṃ kilomakaṃ pihakaṃ papphāsaṃ antaṃ antaguṇaṃ udariyaṃ karīsaṃ pittaṃ semhaṃ pubbo lohitaṃ sedo medo assu vasā kheḷo siṅghāṇikā lasikā muttaṃ' ti.

D. Section on Reflections on Repulsiveness

Again, monks, a monk reflects on this very body, that is covered with skin and full of impurities of all kinds from the soles of the feet upwards and from the hair of the head downwards, considering thus: "In this body, there are hairs of the head, hairs of the skin, nails, teeth, skin, flesh, sinews, bones, marrow, kidney, heart, liver, pleura, spleen, lungs, intestines, mesentery, stomach with its contents, faeces, bile, phlegm, pus, blood, sweat, fat, tears, grease, saliva, nasal mucus, synovial fluid and urine."

Just as if there were a double-mouthed provision bag, full of various kinds of grains and seeds, such as hill-paddy, paddy, mung-beans, cow-peas, sesame seeds and husked rice, and as if there were a man with discerning eyes, who, after having opened that bag would examine the contents, saying: "This is hill-paddy, this is paddy, these are mung-beans, these are cow-peas, these are sesame seeds and this is husked rice"; in this same way, monks, a monk reflects on this very body, that is covered with skin and full of impurities of all kinds from the soles of the feet upwards and from the hair of the head downwards, considering thus: "In this body, there are hairs of the head, hairs of the skin, nails, teeth, skin, flesh, sinews, bones, marrow, kidney, heart, liver, pleura, spleen, lungs, intestines, mesentery, stomach with its contents, faeces, bile, phlegm, pus, blood, sweat, fat, tears, grease, saliva, nasal mucus, synovial fluid and urine."

Iti ajjhattaṃ vā kāye kāyānupassī viharati, bahiddhā vā kāye kāyānupassī viharati, ajjhattabahiddhā vā kāye kāyānupassī viharati, samudayadhammānupassī vā kāyasmiṃ viharati, vayadhammānupassī vā kāyasmiṃ viharati, samudayavaya-dhammānupassī vā kāyasmiṃ viharati, 'atthi kāyo' ti vā panassa sati paccupaṭṭhitā hoti. Yāvadeva ñāṇamattāya paṭissatimattāya anissito ca viharati, na ca kiñci loke upādiyati. Evaṃ pi kho, bhikkhave, bhikkhu kāye kāyānupassī viharati.

E. Dhātumanasikārapabbaṃ

Puna caparaṃ, bhikkhave, bhikkhu imameva kāyaṃ yathāṭhitaṃ yathāpaṇihitaṃ dhātuso paccavekkhati: 'Atthi imasmiṃ kāye pathavīdhātu āpodhātu tejodhātu vāyodhātū' ti.

Seyyathāpi, bhikkhave, dakkho goghātako vā goghātakantevāsī vā gāviṃ vadhitvā catumahāpathe bilaso vibhajitvā nisinno assa; evameva kho, bhikkhave, bhikkhu imameva kāyaṃ yathāṭhitaṃ yathāpaṇihitaṃ dhātuso paccavekkhati: 'Atthi imasmiṃ kāye pathavīdhātu āpodhātu tejodhātu vāyodhātū' ti.

Iti ajjhattaṃ vā kāye kāyānupassī viharati, bahiddhā vā kāye kāyānupassī viharati, ajjhattabahiddhā vā kāye kāyānupassī viharati, samudayadhammānupassī vā kāyasmiṃ viharati, vayadhammānupassī vā kāyasmiṃ viharati, samudayavaya-dhammānupassī vā kāyasmiṃ viharati, 'atthi kāyo' ti vā panassa sati paccupaṭṭhitā hoti. Yāvadeva ñāṇamattāya paṭissatimattāya anissito ca viharati, na ca kiñci loke upādiyati. Evaṃ pi kho, bhikkhave, bhikkhu kāye kāyānupassī viharati.

Thus he dwells observing body in body internally, or he dwells observing body in body externally, or he dwells observing body in body both internally and externally. Thus he dwells observing the phenomenon of arising in the body, thus he dwells observing the phenomenon of passing away in the body, thus he dwells observing the phenomenon of arising and passing away in the body. Now his awareness is established: "This is body!" Thus he develops his awareness to such an extent that there is mere understanding along with mere awareness. In this way he dwells detached, without clinging towards anything in the world [of mind and matter]. This is how, monks, a monk dwells observing body in body.

E. Section on the Reflections on the Material Elements

Again, monks, a monk reflects on this very body, however it is placed or disposed, considering it according to the characteristic of each element: "In this body, there is the earth-element, the water-element, the fire-element and the air-element."

Just as if, monks, a skilful cow-butcher or his apprentice, after having slaughtered a cow and having divided it into portions, would sit down at the junction of four roads; in the same way, monks, a monk reflects on this very body, however it is placed or disposed, considering the material elements: "In this body, there is the earth-element, the water-element, the fire-element and the air-element."

Thus he dwells observing body in body internally, or he dwells observing body in body externally, or he dwells observing body in body both internally and externally. Thus he dwells observing the phenomenon of arising in the body, thus he dwells observing the phenomenon of passing away in the body, thus he dwells observing the phenomenon of arising and passing away in the body. Now his awareness is established: "This is body!" Thus he develops his awareness to such an extent that there is mere understanding along with mere awareness. In this way he dwells detached, without clinging towards anything in the world [of mind and matter]. This is how, monks, a monk dwells observing body in body.

F. Navasivathikapabbaṃ

Puna caparaṃ, bhikkhave, bhikkhu seyyathāpi passeyya sarīraṃ sivathikāya chaḍḍitaṃ ekāhamataṃ vā dvīhamataṃ vā tīhamataṃ vā uddhumātakaṃ vinīlakaṃ vipubbakajātaṃ. So imameva kāyaṃ upasaṃharati: 'ayaṃ pi kho kāyo evaṃdhammo evaṃbhāvī evaṃanatīto' ti.

Iti ajjhattaṃ vā kāye kāyānupassī viharati, bahiddhā vā kāye kāyānupassī viharati, ajjhattabahiddhā vā kāye kāyānupassī viharati, samudayadhammānupassī vā kāyasmiṃ viharati, vayadhammānupassī vā kāyasmiṃ viharati, samudayavaya-dhammānupassī vā kāyasmiṃ viharati, 'atthi kāyo' ti vā panassa sati paccupaṭṭhitā hoti. Yāvadeva ñāṇamattāya paṭissatimattāya anissito ca viharati, na ca kiñci loke upādiyati. Evaṃ pi kho, bhikkhave, bhikkhu kāye kāyānupassī viharati.

Puna caparaṃ, bhikkhave, bhikkhu seyyathāpi passeyya sarīraṃ sivathikāya chaḍḍitaṃ kākehi vā khajjamānaṃ kulalehi vā khajjamānaṃ gijjhehi vā khajjamānaṃ kaṅkehi vā khajjamānaṃ sunakhehi vā khajjamānaṃ byagghehi vā khajjamānaṃ dīpīhi vā khajjamānaṃ siṅgālehi vā khajjamānaṃ vividhehi vā pāṇakajātehi khajjamānaṃ. So imameva kāyaṃ upasaṃharati: 'ayaṃ pi kho kāyo evaṃdhammo evaṃbhāvī evaṃanatīto' ti.

F. Section on the Nine Charnel-ground Observations

Again, monks, a monk, when he sees a dead body that has been thrown in a charnel-ground, dead for one, two or three days, swollen, blue and festering, regarding his own body considers thus: "Indeed, this body is of the same nature, it will become like that and cannot escape it."

Thus he dwells observing body in body internally, or he dwells observing body in body externally, or he dwells observing body in body both internally and externally. Thus he dwells observing the phenomenon of arising in the body, thus he dwells observing the phenomenon of passing away in the body, thus he dwells observing the phenomenon of arising and passing away in the body. Now his awareness is established: "This is body!" Thus he develops his awareness to such an extent that there is mere understanding along with mere awareness. In this way he dwells detached, without clinging towards anything in the world [of mind and matter]. This is how, monks, a monk dwells observing body in body.

Again, monks, a monk, when he sees a dead body that has been thrown in a charnel-ground, being eaten by crows, being eaten by vultures, being eaten by falcons, being eaten by herons, being eaten by dogs, being eaten by tigers, being eaten by leopards, being eaten by jackals and being eaten by different kinds of creatures, regarding his own body considers thus: "Indeed, this body is of the same nature, it will become like that and cannot escape it."

Iti ajjhattaṃ vā kāye kāyānupassī viharati, bahiddhā vā kāye kāyānupassī viharati, ajjhattabahiddhā vā kāye kāyānupassī viharati, samudayadhammānupassī vā kāyasmiṃ viharati, vayadhammānupassī vā kāyasmiṃ viharati, samudayavaya-dhammānupassī vā kāyasmiṃ viharati, 'atthi kāyo' ti vā panassa sati paccupaṭṭhitā hoti. Yāvadeva ñāṇamattāya paṭissatimattāya anissito ca viharati, na ca kiñci loke upādiyati. Evaṃ pi kho, bhikkhave, bhikkhu kāye kāyānupassī viharati.

Puna caparaṃ, bhikkhave, bhikkhu seyyathāpi passeyya sarīraṃ sivathikāya chaḍḍitaṃ aṭṭhikasaṅkhalikaṃ samaṃsalohitaṃ nhārusambandhaṃ. So imameva kāyaṃ upasaṃharati: 'ayaṃ pi kho kāyo evaṃdhammo evaṃbhāvī evaṃanatīto' ti.

Iti ajjhattaṃ vā kāye kāyānupassī viharati, bahiddhā vā kāye kāyānupassī viharati, ajjhattabahiddhā vā kāye kāyānupassī viharati, samudayadhammānupassī vā kāyasmiṃ viharati, vayadhammānupassī vā kāyasmiṃ viharati, samudayavaya-dhammānupassī vā kāyasmiṃ viharati, 'atthi kāyo' ti vā panassa sati paccupaṭṭhitā hoti. Yāvadeva ñāṇamattāya paṭissatimattāya anissito ca viharati, na ca kiñci loke upādiyati. Evaṃ pi kho, bhikkhave, bhikkhu kāye kāyānupassī viharati.

Thus he dwells observing body in body internally, or he dwells observing body in body externally, or he dwells observing body in body both internally and externally. Thus he dwells observing the phenomenon of arising in the body, thus he dwells observing the phenomenon of passing away in the body, thus he dwells observing the phenomenon of arising and passing away in the body. Now his awareness is established: "This is body!" Thus he develops his awareness to such an extent that there is mere understanding along with mere awareness. In this way he dwells detached, without clinging towards anything in the world [of mind and matter]. This is how, monks, a monk dwells observing body in body.

Again, monks, a monk, when he sees a dead body that has been thrown in a charnel-ground, reduced to a skeleton with some flesh and blood attached to it and held together by tendons, regarding his own body considers thus: "Indeed, this body is of the same nature, it will become like that and cannot escape it."

Thus he dwells observing body in body internally, or he dwells observing body in body externally, or he dwells observing body in body both internally and externally. Thus he dwells observing the phenomenon of arising in the body, thus he dwells observing the phenomenon of passing away in the body, thus he dwells observing the phenomenon of arising and passing away in the body. Now his awareness is established: "This is body!" Thus he develops his awareness to such an extent that there is mere understanding along with mere awareness. In this way he dwells detached, without clinging towards anything in the world [of mind and matter]. This is how, monks, a monk dwells observing body in body.

Puna caparaṃ, bhikkhave, bhikkhu seyyathāpi passeyya sarīraṃ sivathikāya chaḍḍitaṃ aṭṭhikasaṅkhalikaṃ nimaṃsalohitamakkhitaṃ nhārusambandhaṃ. So imameva kāyaṃ upasaṃharati: 'ayaṃ pi kho kāyo evaṃdhammo evaṃbhāvī evaṃanatīto' ti.

Iti ajjhattaṃ vā kāye kāyānupassī viharati, bahiddhā vā kāye kāyānupassī viharati, ajjhattabahiddhā vā kāye kāyānupassī viharati, samudayadhammānupassī vā kāyasmiṃ viharati, vayadhammānupassī vā kāyasmiṃ viharati, samudayavaya-dhammānupassī vā kāyasmiṃ viharati, 'atthi kāyo' ti vā panassa sati paccupaṭṭhitā hoti. Yāvadeva ñāṇamattāya paṭissatimattāya anissito ca viharati, na ca kiñci loke upādiyati. Evaṃ pi kho, bhikkhave, bhikkhu kāye kāyānupassī viharati.

Puna caparaṃ, bhikkhave, bhikkhu seyyathāpi passeyya sarīraṃ sivathikāya chaḍḍitaṃ aṭṭhikasaṅkhalikaṃ apagatamaṃsalohitaṃ nhārusambandhaṃ. So imameva kāyaṃ upasaṃharati: 'ayaṃ pi kho kāyo evaṃdhammo evaṃbhāvī evaṃanatīto' ti.

Iti ajjhattaṃ vā kāye kāyānupassī viharati, bahiddhā vā kāye kāyānupassī viharati, ajjhattabahiddhā vā kāye kāyānupassī viharati, samudayadhammānupassī vā kāyasmiṃ viharati, vayadhammānupassī vā kāyasmiṃ viharati, samudayavaya-dhammānupassī vā kāyasmiṃ viharati, 'atthi kāyo' ti vā panassa sati paccupaṭṭhitā hoti. Yāvadeva ñāṇamattāya paṭissatimattāya anissito ca viharati, na ca kiñci loke upādiyati. Evaṃ pi kho, bhikkhave, bhikkhu kāye kāyānupassī viharati.

Again, monks, a monk, when he sees a dead body that has been thrown in a charnel-ground, reduced to a skeleton without any flesh but smeared with blood and held together by tendons, regarding his own body considers thus: "Indeed, this body is of the same nature, it will become like that and cannot escape it."

Thus he dwells observing body in body internally, or he dwells observing body in body externally, or he dwells observing body in body both internally and externally. Thus he dwells observing the phenomenon of arising in the body, thus he dwells observing the phenomenon of passing away in the body, thus he dwells observing the phenomenon of arising and passing away in the body. Now his awareness is established: "This is body!" Thus he develops his awareness to such an extent that there is mere understanding along with mere awareness. In this way he dwells detached, without clinging towards anything in the world [of mind and matter]. This is how, monks, a monk dwells observing body in body.

Again, monks, a monk, when he sees a dead body that has been thrown in a charnel-ground, reduced to a skeleton without any flesh or blood, held together by tendons, regarding his own body considers thus: "Indeed, this body is of the same nature, it will become like that and cannot escape it."

Thus he dwells observing body in body internally, or he dwells observing body in body externally, or he dwells observing body in body both internally and externally. Thus he dwells observing the phenomenon of arising in the body, thus he dwells observing the phenomenon of passing away in the body, thus he dwells observing the phenomenon of arising and passing away in the body. Now his awareness is established: "This is body!" Thus he develops his awareness to such an extent that there is mere understanding along with mere awareness. In this way he dwells detached, without clinging towards anything in the world [of mind and matter]. This is how, monks, a monk dwells observing body in body.

Puna caparaṃ, bhikkhave, bhikkhu seyyathāpi passeyya sarīraṃ sivathikāya chaḍḍitaṃ aṭṭhikāni apagatasambandhāni disā vidisā vikkhittāni, aññena hatthaṭṭhikaṃ aññena pādaṭṭhikaṃ aññena gopphakaṭṭhikaṃ aññena jaṅghaṭṭhikaṃ aññena ūruṭṭhikaṃ aññena kaṭiṭṭhikaṃ aññena phāsukaṭṭhikaṃ aññena piṭṭhiṭṭhikaṃ aññena khandhaṭṭhikaṃ aññena gīvaṭṭhikaṃ aññena hanukaṭṭhikaṃ aññena dantaṭṭhikaṃ aññena sīsakaṭāhaṃ. So imameva kāyaṃ upasaṃharati: 'ayaṃ pi kho kāyo evaṃdhammo evaṃbhāvī evaṃanatīto' ti.

Iti ajjhattaṃ vā kāye kāyānupassī viharati, bahiddhā vā kāye kāyānupassī viharati, ajjhattabahiddhā vā kāye kāyānupassī viharati, samudayadhammānupassī vā kāyasmiṃ viharati, vayadhammānupassī vā kāyasmiṃ viharati, samudayavaya-dhammānupassī vā kāyasmiṃ viharati, 'atthi kāyo' ti vā panassa sati paccupaṭṭhitā hoti. Yāvadeva ñāṇamattāya paṭissatimattāya anissito ca viharati, na ca kiñci loke upādiyati. Evaṃ pi kho, bhikkhave, bhikkhu kāye kāyānupassī viharati.

Puna caparaṃ, bhikkhave, bhikkhu seyyathāpi passeyya sarīraṃ sivathikāya chaḍḍitaṃ aṭṭhikāni setāni saṅkhavaṇṇapaṭibhāgāni. So imameva kāyaṃ upasaṃharati: 'ayaṃ pi kho kāyo evaṃdhammo evaṃbhāvī evaṃanatīto' ti.

Again, monks, a monk, when he sees a dead body that has been thrown in a charnel-ground, reduced to disconnected bones, scattered in all directions, here a bone of the hand, there a bone of the foot, here a bone of the ankle, there a bone of the knee, here a bone of the thigh and there a bone of the pelvis, here a bone of the ribs, there a bone of the spine, again there a bone of the shoulder, here a bone of the throat, there a bone of the chin, here a bone of the teeth and there a bone of the skull, regarding his own body considers thus: "Indeed, this body is of the same nature, it will become like that and cannot escape it."

Thus he dwells observing body in body internally, or he dwells observing body in body externally, or he dwells observing body in body both internally and externally. Thus he dwells observing the phenomenon of arising in the body, thus he dwells observing the phenomenon of passing away in the body, thus he dwells observing the phenomenon of arising and passing away in the body. Now his awareness is established: "This is body!" Thus he develops his awareness to such an extent that there is mere understanding along with mere awareness. In this way he dwells detached, without clinging towards anything in the world [of mind and matter]. This is how, monks, a monk dwells observing body in body.

Again, monks, a monk, when he sees a dead body that has been thrown in a charnel-ground, reduced to bleached bones of conch-like colour, regarding his own body considers thus: "Indeed, this body is of the same nature, it will become like that and cannot escape it."

Iti ajjhattaṃ vā kāye kāyānupassī viharati, bahiddhā vā kāye kāyānupassī viharati, ajjhattabahiddhā vā kāye kāyānupassī viharati, samudayadhammānupassī vā kāyasmiṃ viharati, vayadhammānupassī vā kāyasmiṃ viharati, samudayavaya-dhammānupassī vā kāyasmiṃ viharati, 'atthi kāyo' ti vā panassa sati paccupaṭṭhitā hoti. Yāvadeva ñāṇamattāya paṭissatimattāya anissito ca viharati, na ca kiñci loke upādiyati. Evaṃ pi kho, bhikkhave, bhikkhu kāye kāyānupassī viharati.

Puna caparaṃ, bhikkhave, bhikkhu seyyathāpi passeyya sarīraṃ sivathikāya chaḍḍitaṃ aṭṭhikāni puñjakitāni terovassikāni. So imameva kāyaṃ upasaṃharati: 'ayaṃ pi kho kāyo evaṃdhammo evaṃbhāvī evaṃanatīto' ti.

Iti ajjhattaṃ vā kāye kāyānupassī viharati, bahiddhā vā kāye kāyānupassī viharati, ajjhattabahiddhā vā kāye kāyānupassī viharati, samudayadhammānupassī vā kāyasmiṃ viharati, vayadhammānupassī vā kāyasmiṃ viharati, samudayavaya-dhammānupassī vā kāyasmiṃ viharati, 'atthi kāyo' ti vā panassa sati paccupaṭṭhitā hoti. Yāvadeva ñāṇamattāya paṭissatimattāya anissito ca viharati, na ca kiñci loke upādiyati. Evaṃ pi kho, bhikkhave, bhikkhu kāye kāyānupassī viharati.

Puna caparaṃ, bhikkhave, bhikkhu seyyathāpi passeyya sarīraṃ sivathikāya chaḍḍitaṃ aṭṭhikāni pūtīni cuṇṇakajātāni. So imameva kāyaṃ upasaṃharati: 'ayaṃ pi kho kāyo evaṃdhammo evaṃbhāvī evaṃanatīto' ti.

Thus he dwells observing body in body internally, or he dwells observing body in body externally, or he dwells observing body in body both internally and externally. Thus he dwells observing the phenomenon of arising in the body, thus he dwells observing the phenomenon of passing away in the body, thus he dwells observing the phenomenon of arising and passing away in the body. Now his awareness is established: "This is body!" Thus he develops his awareness to such an extent that there is mere understanding along with mere awareness. In this way he dwells detached, without clinging towards anything in the world [of mind and matter]. This is how, monks, a monk dwells observing body in body.

Again, monks, a monk, when he sees a dead body that has been thrown in a charnel-ground, of bones that are piled up in a heap more than a year old, regarding his own body considers thus: "Indeed, this body is of the same nature, it will become like that and cannot escape it."

Thus he dwells observing body in body internally, or he dwells observing body in body externally, or he dwells observing body in body both internally and externally. Thus he dwells observing the phenomenon of arising in the body, thus he dwells observing the phenomenon of passing away in the body, thus he dwells observing the phenomenon of arising and passing away in the body. Now his awareness is established: "This is body!" Thus he develops his awareness to such an extent that there is mere understanding along with mere awareness. In this way he dwells detached, without clinging towards anything in the world [of mind and matter]. This is how, monks, a monk dwells observing body in body.

Again, monks, a monk, when he sees a dead body that has been thrown in a charnel-ground, the bones having rotted away to powder, regarding his own body considers thus: "Indeed, this body is of the same nature, it will become like that and cannot escape it."

Iti ajjhattaṃ vā kāye kāyānupassī viharati, bahiddhā vā kāye kāyānupassī viharati, ajjhattabahiddhā vā kāye kāyānupassī viharati, samudayadhammānupassī vā kāyasmiṃ viharati, vayadhammānupassī vā kāyasmiṃ viharati, samudayavaya-dhammānupassī vā kāyasmiṃ viharati, 'atthi kāyo' ti vā panassa sati paccupaṭṭhitā hoti. Yāvadeva ñāṇamattāya paṭissatimattāya anissito ca viharati, na ca kiñci loke upādiyati. Evaṃ pi kho, bhikkhave, bhikkhu kāye kāyānupassī viharati.

Thus he dwells observing body in body internally, or he dwells observing body in body externally, or he dwells observing body in body both internally and externally. Thus he dwells observing the phenomenon of arising in the body, thus he dwells observing the phenomenon of passing away in the body, thus he dwells observing the phenomenon of arising and passing away in the body. Now his awareness is established: "This is body!" Thus he develops his awareness to such an extent that there is mere understanding along with mere awareness. In this way he dwells detached, without clinging towards anything in the world [of mind and matter]. This is how, monks, a monk dwells observing body in body.

3. Vedanānupassanā

Kathaṃ ca pana, bhikkhave, bhikkhu vedanāsu vedanānupassī viharati?

Idha, bhikkhave, bhikkhu sukhaṃ vā vedanaṃ vedayamāno 'sukhaṃ vedanaṃ vedayāmī' ti pajānāti; dukkhaṃ vā vedanaṃ vedayamāno 'dukkhaṃ vedanaṃ vedayāmī' ti pajānāti; adukkhamasukhaṃ vā vedanaṃ vedayamāno 'adukkham-asukhaṃ vedanaṃ vedayāmī' ti pajānāti. Sāmisaṃ vā sukhaṃ vedanaṃ vedayamāno 'sāmisaṃ sukhaṃ vedanaṃ vedayāmī' ti pajānāti; nirāmisaṃ vā sukhaṃ vedanaṃ vedayamāno 'nirāmisaṃ sukhaṃ vedanaṃ vedayāmī' ti pajānāti. Sāmisaṃ vā dukkhaṃ vedanaṃ vedayamāno 'sāmisaṃ dukkhaṃ vedanaṃ vedayāmī' ti pajānāti; nirāmisaṃ vā dukkhaṃ vedanaṃ vedayamāno 'nirāmisaṃ dukkhaṃ vedanaṃ vedayāmī' ti pajānāti. Sāmisaṃ vā adukkhamasukhaṃ vedanaṃ vedayamāno 'sāmisaṃ adukkhamasukhaṃ vedanaṃ vedayāmī' ti pajānāti; nirāmisaṃ vā adukkhamasukhaṃ vedanaṃ vedayamāno 'nirāmisaṃ adukkhamasukhaṃ vedanaṃ vedayāmī' ti pajānāti.[12]

3. The Observation of Sensations

How, monks, does a monk dwell, observing sensations in sensations?

Here, monks, a monk, while experiencing a pleasant sensation, understands properly, "I am experiencing a pleasant sensation"; while experiencing an unpleasant sensation, he understands properly, "I am experiencing an unpleasant sensation"; while experiencing a neither-unpleasant-nor-pleasant sensation, he understands properly, "I am experiencing a neither-unpleasant-nor-pleasant sensation." While he is experiencing a pleasant sensation with attachment, he understands properly, "I am experiencing a pleasant sensation with attachment"; while he is experiencing a pleasant sensation without attachment, he understands properly, "I am experiencing a pleasant sensation without attachment"; while experiencing an unpleasant sensation with attachment, he understands properly, "I am experiencing an unpleasant sensation with attachment"; while experiencing an unpleasant sensation without attachment, he understands properly, "I am experiencing an unpleasant sensation without attachment"; while experiencing a neither-unpleasant-nor-pleasant sensation with attachment, he understands properly, "I am experiencing a neither-unpleasant-nor-pleasant sensation with attachment"; while experiencing a neither-unpleasant-nor-pleasant sensation without attachment, he understands properly, "I am experiencing a neither-unpleasant-nor-pleasant sensation without attachment."[12]

Iti ajjhattaṃ vā vedanāsu vedanānupassī viharati, bahiddhā[13] vā vedanāsu vedanānupassī viharati, ajjhattabahiddhā vā vedanāsu vedanānupassī viharati, samudayadhammānupassī vā vedanāsu viharati, vayadhammānupassī vā vedanāsu viharati, samudayavayadhammānupassī vā vedanāsu viharati, 'atthi vedanā' ti vā panassa sati paccupaṭṭhitā hoti. Yāvadeva ñāṇamattāya paṭissatimattāya anissito ca viharati, na ca kiñci loke upādiyati. Evaṃ pi kho, bhikkhave, bhikkhu vedanāsu vedanānupassī viharati.

4. Cittānupassanā

Kathaṃ ca pana, bhikkhave, bhikkhu citte[14] cittānupassī viharati?

Idha, bhikkhave, bhikkhu sarāgaṃ vā cittaṃ 'sarāgaṃ cittaṃ' ti pajānāti, vītarāgaṃ vā cittaṃ 'vītarāgaṃ cittaṃ' ti pajānāti, sadosaṃ vā cittaṃ 'sadosaṃ cittaṃ' ti pajānāti, vītadosaṃ vā cittaṃ 'vītadosaṃ cittaṃ' ti pajānāti, samohaṃ vā cittaṃ 'samohaṃ cittaṃ' ti pajānāti, vītamohaṃ vā cittaṃ 'vītamohaṃ cittaṃ' ti pajānāti, saṅkhittaṃ vā cittaṃ 'saṅkhittaṃ cittaṃ' ti pajānāti, vikkhittaṃ vā cittaṃ 'vikkhittaṃ cittaṃ'[15] ti pajānāti, mahaggataṃ vā cittaṃ 'mahaggataṃ cittaṃ' ti pajānāti, amahaggataṃ vā cittaṃ 'amahaggataṃ cittaṃ'[16] ti pajānāti, sa-uttaraṃ vā cittaṃ 'sa-uttaraṃ cittaṃ' ti pajānāti, anuttaraṃ vā cittaṃ 'anuttaraṃ cittaṃ'[17] ti pajānāti, samāhitaṃ vā cittaṃ 'samāhitaṃ cittaṃ' ti pajānāti, asamāhitaṃ vā cittaṃ 'asamāhitaṃ cittaṃ'[18] ti pajānāti, vimuttaṃ vā cittaṃ 'vimuttaṃ cittaṃ' ti pajānāti, avimuttaṃ vā cittaṃ 'avimuttaṃ cittaṃ' ti pajānāti.

Thus he dwells observing sensations in sensations internally, or he dwells observing sensations in sensations externally,[13] or he dwells observing sensations in sensations both internally and externally. Thus he dwells observing the phenomenon of arising in sensations, thus he dwells observing the phenomenon of passing away in sensations, thus he dwells observing the phenomenon of arising and passing away in sensations. Now his awareness is established: "This is sensation!" Thus he develops his awareness to such an extent that there is mere understanding along with mere awareness. In this way he dwells detached, without clinging towards anything in the world [of mind and matter]. This is how, monks, a monk dwells observing sensations in sensations.

4. The Observation of Mind

Again, monks, how does a monk dwell, observing mind in mind?[14]

Here, monks, a monk understands properly mind with craving as mind with craving, he understands properly mind free from craving as mind free from craving, he understands properly mind with aversion as mind with aversion, he understands properly mind free from aversion as mind free from aversion, he understands properly mind with delusion as mind with delusion, he understands properly mind free from delusion as mind free from delusion, he understands properly collected mind as collected mind, he understands properly a scattered mind as scattered mind,[15] he understands properly expanded mind as expanded mind, he understands properly unexpanded mind as unexpanded mind,[16] he understands properly surpassable mind as surpassable mind, he understands properly unsurpassable mind as unsurpassable mind,[17] he understands properly concentrated mind as concentrated mind, he understands properly unconcentrated mind as unconcentrated mind,[18] he understands properly freed mind as freed mind, he understands properly not freed mind as not freed mind.

Iti ajjhattaṃ vā citte cittānupassī viharati, bahiddhā vā citte cittānupassī viharati, ajjhattabahiddhā vā citte cittānupassī viharati,[19] samudayadhammānupassī vā cittasmiṃ viharati, vayadhammānupassī vā cittasmiṃ viharati, samudayavaya-dhammānupassī vā cittasmiṃ viharati, 'atthi cittaṃ' ti vā panassa sati paccupaṭṭhitā hoti. Yāvadeva ñāṇamattāya paṭissatimattāya anissito ca viharati, na ca kiñci loke upādiyati. Evaṃ pi kho, bhikkhave, bhikkhu citte cittānupassī viharati.

5. Dhammānupassanā

A. Nīvaraṇapabbaṃ

Kathaṃ ca pana, bhikkhave, bhikkhu dhammesu dhammānupassī viharati?

Idha, bhikkhave, bhikkhu dhammesu dhammānupassī viharati—pañcasu nīvaraṇesu.

Kathaṃ ca pana, bhikkhave, bhikkhu dhammesu dhammānupassī viharati—pañcasu nīvaraṇesu?

Idha, bhikkhave, bhikkhu santaṃ vā ajjhattaṃ kāmacchandaṃ 'atthi me ajjhattaṃ kāmacchando' ti pajānāti, asantaṃ vā ajjhattaṃ kāmacchandaṃ 'natthi me ajjhattaṃ kāmacchando' ti pajānāti, yathā ca anuppannassa kāmacchandassa uppādo hoti taṃ ca pajānāti, yathā ca uppannassa kāmacchandassa pahānaṃ hoti taṃ ca pajānāti, yathā ca pahīnassa kāmacchandassa āyatiṃ anuppādo hoti taṃ ca pajānāti.

Thus he dwells observing mind in mind internally, or he dwells observing mind in mind externally, or he dwells observing mind in mind both internally and externally.[19] Thus he dwells observing the phenomenon of arising in the mind, thus he dwells observing the phenomenon of passing away in the mind, thus he dwells observing the phenomenon of arising and passing away in the mind. Now his awareness is established: "This is mind!" Thus he develops his awareness to such an extent that there is mere understanding along with mere awareness. In this way he dwells detached, without clinging towards anything in the world [of mind and matter]. This is how, monks, a monk dwells observing mind in mind.

5. The Observation of Mental Contents

A. The Section on the Hindrances

Again, monks, how does a monk dwell, observing mental contents in mental contents?

Here, monks, a monk dwells, observing mental contents in mental contents, as regards the five hindrances.

How, monks, does a monk dwell, observing mental contents in mental contents, as regards the five hindrances?

Here, monks, a monk, whenever sense desire is present in him, he understands properly that, "Sense desire is present in me." Whenever sense desire is absent from him, he understands properly that, "Sense desire is absent from me." He understands properly, how sense desire that has not yet arisen in him, comes to arise. He understands properly, how sense desire that has now arisen in him, gets eradicated. He understands properly, how sense desire that has now been eradicated, will in future no longer arise in him.

Santaṃ vā ajjhattaṃ byāpādaṃ 'atthi me ajjhattaṃ byāpādo' ti pajānāti, asantaṃ vā ajjhattaṃ byāpādaṃ 'natthi me ajjhattaṃ byāpādo' ti pajānāti, yathā ca anuppannassa byāpādassa uppādo hoti taṃ ca pajānāti, yathā ca uppannassa byāpādassa pahānaṃ hoti taṃ ca pajānāti, yathā ca pahīnassa byāpādassa āyatiṃ anuppādo hoti taṃ ca pajānāti.

Santaṃ vā ajjhattaṃ thinamiddhaṃ 'atthi me ajjhattaṃ thinamiddhaṃ' ti pajānāti, asantaṃ vā ajjhattaṃ thinamiddhaṃ 'natthi me ajjhattaṃ thinamiddhaṃ' ti pajānāti, yathā ca anuppannassa thinamiddhassa uppādo hoti taṃ ca pajānāti, yathā ca uppannassa thinamiddhassa pahānaṃ hoti taṃ ca pajānāti, yathā ca pahīnassa thinamiddhassa āyatiṃ anuppādo hoti taṃ ca pajānāti.

Santaṃ vā ajjhattaṃ uddhaccakukkuccaṃ 'atthi me ajjhattaṃ uddhaccakukkuccaṃ' ti pajānāti, asantaṃ vā ajjhattaṃ uddhaccakukkuccaṃ 'natthi me ajjhattaṃ uddhaccakukkuccaṃ' ti pajānāti, yathā ca anuppannassa uddhaccakukkuccassa uppādo hoti taṃ ca pajānāti, yathā ca uppannassa uddhaccakukkuccassa pahānaṃ hoti taṃ ca pajānāti, yathā ca pahīnassa uddhaccakukkuccassa āyatiṃ anuppādo hoti taṃ ca pajānāti.

Santaṃ vā ajjhattaṃ vicikicchaṃ 'atthi me ajjhattaṃ vicikicchā' ti pajānāti, asantaṃ vā ajjhattaṃ vicikicchaṃ 'natthi me ajjhattaṃ vicikicchā' ti pajānāti, yathā ca anuppannāya vicikicchāya uppādo hoti taṃ ca pajānāti, yathā ca uppannāya vicikicchāya pahānaṃ hoti taṃ ca pajānāti, yathā ca pahīnāya vicikicchāya āyatiṃ anuppādo hoti taṃ ca pajānāti.

Whenever aversion is present in him, he understands properly that, "Aversion is present in me." Whenever aversion is absent from him, he understands properly that, "Aversion is absent from me." He understands properly, how aversion that has not yet arisen in him, comes to arise. He understands properly, how aversion that has now arisen in him, gets eradicated. He understands properly, how aversion that has now been eradicated, will in future no longer arise in him.

Whenever sloth and torpor are present in him, he understands properly that, "Sloth and torpor are present in me." Whenever sloth and torpor are absent from him, he understands properly that, "Sloth and torpor are absent from me." He understands properly, how sloth and torpor that have not yet arisen in him, come to arise. He understands properly, how sloth and torpor that have now arisen in him, get eradicated. He understands properly, how sloth and torpor that have now been eradicated, will in future no longer arise in him.

Whenever agitation and remorse are present in him, he understands properly that, "Agitation and remorse are present in me." Whenever agitation and remorse are absent from him, he understands properly that, "Agitation and remorse are absent from me." He understands properly, how agitation and remorse that have not yet arisen in him, come to arise. He understands properly, how agitation and remorse that have now arisen in him, get eradicated. He understands properly, how agitation and remorse that have now been eradicated, will in future no longer arise in him.

Whenever doubt is present in him, he understands properly that, "Doubt is present in me." Whenever doubt is absent from him, he understands properly that, "Doubt is absent from me." He understands properly, how doubt that has not yet arisen in him, comes to arise. He understands properly, how doubt that has now arisen in him, gets eradicated. He understands properly, how doubt that has now been eradicated, will in future no longer arise in him.

Iti ajjhattaṃ vā dhammesu dhammānupassī viharati, bahiddhā vā dhammesu dhammānupassī viharati, ajjhattabahiddhā vā dhammesu dhammānupassī viharati, samudayadhammānupassī vā dhammesu viharati, vayadhammānupassī vā dhammesu viharati, samudayavaya-dhammānupassī vā dhammesu viharati, 'atthi dhammā' ti vā panassa sati paccupaṭṭhitā hoti. Yāvadeva ñāṇamattāya paṭissatimattāya anissito ca viharati, na ca kiñci loke upādiyati. Evaṃ pi kho, bhikkhave, bhikkhu dhammesu dhammānupassī viharati pañcasu nīvaraṇesu.

B. Khandhapabbaṃ

Puna caparaṃ, bhikkhave, bhikkhu dhammesu dhammānupassī viharati pañcasu upādānakkhandhesu.[20]

Kathaṃ ca pana, bhikkhave, bhikkhu dhammesu dhammānupassī viharati pañcasu upādānakkhandhesu?

Idha, bhikkhave, bhikkhu, 'iti rūpaṃ, iti rūpassa samudayo, iti rūpassa atthaṅgamo; iti vedanā, iti vedanāya samudayo, iti vedanāya atthaṅgamo; iti saññā, iti saññāya samudayo, iti saññāya atthaṅgamo; iti saṅkhārā, iti saṅkhārānaṃ samudayo, iti saṅkhārānaṃ atthaṅgamo; iti viññāṇaṃ, iti viññāṇassa samudayo, iti viññāṇassa atthaṅgamo' ti.

Thus he dwells observing mental contents in mental contents internally, or he dwells observing mental contents in mental contents externally, or he dwells observing mental contents in mental contents both internally and externally. Thus he dwells observing the phenomenon of arising in the mental contents, thus he dwells observing the phenomenon of passing away in the mental contents, thus he dwells observing the phenomenon of arising and passing away in the mental contents. Now his awareness is established: "These are mental contents!" Thus he develops his awareness to such an extent that there is mere understanding along with mere awareness. In this way he dwells detached, without clinging towards anything in the world [of mind and matter]. This is how, monks, a monk dwells observing mental contents in mental contents as regards the five hindrances.

B. The Section on the Aggregates

Again, monks, a monk dwells, observing mental contents in mental contents, as regards the five aggregates of clinging.[20]

How, monks, does a monk dwell, observing mental contents in mental contents, as regards the five aggregates of clinging?

Here, monks, a monk [understands properly]: "Such is matter, such is the arising of matter, such is the passing away of matter; such are sensations, such is the arising of sensations, such is the passing away of sensations; such is perception, such is the arising of perception, such is the passing away of perception; such are reactions, such is the arising of reactions, such is the passing away of reactions; such is consciousness, such is the arising of consciousness, such is the passing away of consciousness."

Iti ajjhattaṃ vā dhammesu dhammānupassī viharati, bahiddhā vā dhammesu dhammānupassī viharati, ajjhattabahiddhā vā dhammesu dhammānupassī viharati, samudayadhammānupassī vā dhammesu viharati, vayadhammānupassī vā dhammesu viharati, samudayavaya-dhammānupassī vā dhammesu viharati, 'atthi dhammā' ti vā panassa sati paccupaṭṭhitā hoti. Yāvadeva ñāṇamattāya paṭissatimattāya anissito ca viharati, na ca kiñci loke upādiyati. Evaṃ pi kho, bhikkhave, bhikkhu dhammesu dhammānupassī viharati pañcasu upādānakkhandhesu.

C. Āyatanapabbaṃ

Puna caparaṃ, bhikkhave, bhikkhu dhammesu dhammānupassī viharati chasu ajjhattikabāhiresu āyatanesu.

Kathaṃ ca pana, bhikkhave, bhikkhu dhammesu dhammānupassī viharati chasu ajjhattikabāhiresu āyatanesu?

Idha, bhikkhave, bhikkhu cakkhuṃ ca pajānāti, rūpe ca pajānāti, yaṃ ca tadubhayaṃ paṭicca uppajjati saṃyojanaṃ taṃ ca pajānāti, yathā ca anuppannassa saṃyojanassa uppādo hoti taṃ ca pajānāti, yathā ca uppannassa saṃyojanassa pahānaṃ hoti taṃ ca pajānāti, yathā ca pahīnassa saṃyojanassa āyatiṃ anuppādo hoti taṃ ca pajānāti.

Thus he dwells observing mental contents in mental contents internally, or he dwells observing mental contents in mental contents externally, or he dwells observing mental contents in mental contents both internally and externally. Thus he dwells observing the phenomenon of arising in the mental contents, thus he dwells observing the phenomenon of passing away in the mental contents, thus he dwells observing the phenomenon of arising and passing away in the mental contents. Now his awareness is established: "These are mental contents!" Thus he develops his awareness to such an extent that there is mere understanding along with mere awareness. In this way he dwells detached, without clinging towards anything in the world [of mind and matter]. This is how, monks, a monk dwells observing mental contents in mental contents as regards the five aggregates of clinging.

C. The Section on the Sense Spheres

Again, monks, a monk dwells, observing mental contents in mental contents, as regards the six internal and external sense spheres.

How, monks, does a monk dwell, observing mental contents in mental contents, as regards the six internal and external sense spheres?

Here, monks, a monk understands properly the eye, he understands properly the visible object and he understands properly the bondage that arises dependent on these two. He understands properly how the bondage that has not yet arisen, comes to arise. He understands properly how the bondage that has now arisen, gets eradicated. He understands properly how that bondage that has now been eradicated, will in future no longer arise.

Sotaṃ ca pajānāti, sadde ca pajānāti, yaṃ ca tadubhayaṃ paṭicca uppajjati saṃyojanaṃ taṃ ca pajānāti, yathā ca anuppannassa saṃyojanassa uppādo hoti taṃ ca pajānāti, yathā ca uppannassa saṃyojanassa pahānaṃ hoti taṃ ca pajānāti, yathā ca pahīnassa saṃyojanassa āyatiṃ anuppādo hoti taṃ ca pajānāti.

Ghānaṃ ca pajānāti, gandhe ca pajānāti, yaṃ ca tadubhayaṃ paṭicca uppajjati saṃyojanaṃ taṃ ca pajānāti, yathā ca anuppannassa saṃyojanassa uppādo hoti taṃ ca pajānāti, yathā ca uppannassa saṃyojanassa pahānaṃ hoti taṃ ca pajānāti, yathā ca pahīnassa saṃyojanassa āyatiṃ anuppādo hoti taṃ ca pajānāti.

Jivhaṃ ca pajānāti, rase ca pajānāti, yaṃ ca tadubhayaṃ paṭicca uppajjati saṃyojanaṃ taṃ ca pajānāti, yathā ca anuppannassa saṃyojanassa uppādo hoti taṃ ca pajānāti, yathā ca uppannassa saṃyojanassa pahānaṃ hoti taṃ ca pajānāti, yathā ca pahīnassa saṃyojanassa āyatiṃ anuppādo hoti taṃ ca pajānāti.

Kāyaṃ ca pajānāti, phoṭṭhabbe ca pajānāti, yaṃ ca tadubhayaṃ paṭicca uppajjati saṃyojanaṃ taṃ ca pajānāti, yathā ca anuppannassa saṃyojanassa uppādo hoti taṃ ca pajānāti, yathā ca uppannassa saṃyojanassa pahānaṃ hoti taṃ ca pajānāti, yathā ca pahīnassa saṃyojanassa āyatiṃ anuppādo hoti taṃ ca pajānāti.

He understands properly the ear, he understands properly sound and he understands properly the bondage that arises dependent on these two. He understands properly how the bondage that has not yet arisen, comes to arise. He understands properly how the bondage that has now arisen, gets eradicated. He understands properly how that bondage that has now been eradicated, will in future no longer arise.

He understands properly the nose, he understands properly smell and he understands properly the bondage that arises dependent on these two. He understands properly how the bondage that has not yet arisen, comes to arise. He understands properly how the bondage that has now arisen, gets eradicated. He understands properly how that bondage that has now been eradicated, will in future no longer arise.

He understands properly the tongue, he understands properly taste and he understands properly the bondage that arises dependent on these two. He understands properly how the bondage that has not yet arisen, comes to arise. He understands properly how the bondage that has now arisen, gets eradicated. He understands properly how that bondage that has now been eradicated, will in future no longer arise.

He understands properly the body, he understands properly touch and he understands properly the bondage that arises dependent on these two. He understands properly how the bondage that has not yet arisen, comes to arise. He understands properly how the bondage that has now arisen, gets eradicated. He understands properly how that bondage that has now been eradicated, will in future no longer arise.

Manaṃ ca pajānāti, dhamme ca pajānāti, yaṃ ca tadubhayaṃ paṭicca uppajjati saṃyojanaṃ taṃ ca pajānāti, yathā ca anuppannassa saṃyojanassa uppādo hoti taṃ ca pajānāti, yathā ca uppannassa saṃyojanassa pahānaṃ hoti taṃ ca pajānāti, yathā ca pahīnassa saṃyojanassa āyatiṃ anuppādo hoti taṃ ca pajānāti.

Iti ajjhattaṃ vā dhammesu dhammānupassī viharati, bahiddhā vā dhammesu dhammānupassī viharati, ajjhattabahiddhā vā dhammesu dhammānupassī viharati, samudayadhammānupassī vā dhammesu viharati, vayadhammānupassī vā dhammesu viharati, samudayavaya-dhammānupassī vā dhammesu viharati, 'atthi dhammā' ti vā panassa sati paccupaṭṭhitā hoti. Yāvadeva ñāṇamattāya paṭissatimattāya anissito ca viharati, na ca kiñci loke upādiyati. Evaṃ pi kho, bhikkhave, bhikkhu dhammesu dhammānupassī viharati chasu ajjhattikabāhiresu āyatanesu.

D. Bojjhaṅgapabbaṃ

Puna caparaṃ, bhikkhave, bhikkhu dhammesu dhammānupassī viharati sattasu bojjhaṅgesu.

Kathaṃ ca pana, bhikkhave, bhikkhu dhammesu dhammānupassī viharati sattasu bojjhaṅgesu?

He understands properly the mind, he understands properly the contents of the mind and he understands properly the bondage that arises dependent on these two. He understands properly how the bondage that has not yet arisen, comes to arise. He understands properly how the bondage that has now arisen, gets eradicated. He understands properly how that bondage that has now been eradicated, will in future no longer arise.

Thus he dwells observing mental contents in mental contents internally, or he dwells observing mental contents in mental contents externally, or he dwells observing mental contents in mental contents both internally and externally. Thus he dwells observing the phenomenon of arising in the mental contents, thus he dwells observing the phenomenon of passing away in the mental contents, thus he dwells observing the phenomenon of arising and passing away in the mental contents. Now his awareness is established: "These are mental contents!" Thus he develops his awareness to such an extent that there is mere understanding along with mere awareness. In this way he dwells detached, without clinging towards anything in the world [of mind and matter]. This is how, monks, a monk dwells observing mental contents in mental contents as regards the six internal and external sense spheres.

D. The Section on the Factors of Enlightenment

Again, monks, a monk dwells observing mental contents in mental contents, as regards the seven factors of enlightenment.

How, monks, does a monk dwell observing mental contents in mental contents, as regards the seven factors of enlightenment?

Idha, bhikkhave, bhikkhu santaṃ vā ajjhattaṃ satisambojjhaṅgaṃ 'atthi me ajjhattaṃ satisambojjhaṅgo' ti pajānāti, asantaṃ vā ajjhattaṃ satisambojjhaṅgaṃ 'natthi me ajjhattaṃ satisambojjhaṅgo' ti pajānāti, yathā ca anuppannassa satisambojjhaṅgassa uppādo hoti taṃ ca pajānāti, yathā ca uppannassa satisambojjhaṅgassa bhāvanāya pāripūrī hoti taṃ ca pajānāti.

Santaṃ vā ajjhattaṃ dhammavicayasambojjhaṅgaṃ[21] 'atthi me ajjhattaṃ dhammavicayasambojjhaṅgo'ti pajānāti, asantaṃ vā ajjhattaṃ dhammavicayasambojjhaṅgaṃ 'natthi me ajjhattaṃ dhammavicayasambojjhaṅgo' ti pajānāti, yathā ca anuppannassa dhammavicayasambojjhaṅgassa uppādo hoti taṃ ca pajānāti, yathā ca uppannassa dhammavicayasambojjhaṅgassa bhāvanāya pāripūrī hoti taṃ ca pajānāti.

Santaṃ vā ajjhattaṃ vīriyasambojjhaṅgaṃ 'atthi me ajjhattaṃ vīriyasambojjhaṅgo' ti pajānāti, asantaṃ vā ajjhattaṃ vīriyasambojjhaṅgaṃ 'natthi me ajjhattaṃ vīriyasambojjhaṅgo' ti pajānāti, yathā ca anuppannassa vīriyasambojjhaṅgassa uppādo hoti taṃ ca pajānāti, yathā ca uppannassa vīriyasambojjhaṅgassa bhāvanāya pāripūrī hoti taṃ ca pajānāti.

Here, monks, a monk understands properly that, when the factor of enlightenment, awareness, is present within him, "The factor of enlightenment, awareness, is present in me." He understands properly that, when the factor of enlightenment, awareness, is absent from him, "The factor of enlightenment, awareness, is absent from me." He understands properly, how the factor of enlightenment, awareness, that has not yet arisen in him, comes to arise. He understands properly, how the factor of enlightenment, awareness, that has now arisen, is developed and perfected.

When the factor of enlightenment, investigation of Dhamma,[21] is present in him, he understands properly, "The factor of enlightenment, investigation of Dhamma, is present in me." He understands properly that, when the factor of enlightenment, investigation of Dhamma, is absent from him, "The factor of enlightenment, investigation of Dhamma, is absent from me." He understands properly, how the factor of enlightenment, investigation of Dhamma, that has not yet arisen in him, comes to arise. He understands properly, how the factor of enlightenment, investigation of Dhamma, that has now arisen, is developed and perfected.

When the factor of enlightenment, effort, is present in him, he understands properly, "The factor of enlightenment, effort, is present in me." He understands properly that, when the factor of enlightenment, effort, is absent from him, "The factor of enlightenment, effort, is absent from me." He understands properly, how the factor of enlightenment, effort, that has not yet arisen in him, comes to arise. He understands properly, how the factor of enlightenment, effort, that has now arisen, is developed and perfected.

Santaṃ vā ajjhattaṃ pītisambojjhaṅgaṃ[22] 'atthi me ajjhattaṃ pītisambojjhaṅgo' ti pajānāti, asantaṃ vā ajjhattaṃ pītisambojjhaṅgaṃ 'natthi me ajjhattaṃ pītisambojjhaṅgo' ti pajānāti, yathā ca anuppannassa pītisambojjhaṅgassa uppādo hoti taṃ ca pajānāti, yathā ca uppannassa pītisambojjhaṅgassa bhāvanāya pāripūrī hoti taṃ ca pajānāti.

Santaṃ vā ajjhattaṃ passaddhisambojjhaṅgaṃ[23] 'atthi me ajjhattaṃ passaddhisambojjhaṅgo' ti pajānāti, asantaṃ vā ajjhattaṃ passaddhisambojjhaṅgaṃ 'natthi me ajjhattaṃ passaddhisambojjhaṅgo' ti pajānāti, yathā ca anuppannassa passaddhisambojjhaṅgassa uppādo hoti taṃ ca pajānāti, yathā ca uppannassa passaddhisambojjhaṅgassa bhāvanāya pāripūrī hoti taṃ ca pajānāti.

Santaṃ vā ajjhattaṃ samādhisambojjhaṅgaṃ 'atthi me ajjhattaṃ samādhisambojjhaṅgo' ti pajānāti, asantaṃ vā ajjhattaṃ samādhisambojjhaṅgaṃ 'natthi me ajjhattaṃ samādhisambojjhaṅgo' ti pajānāti, yathā ca anuppannassa samādhisambojjhaṅgassa uppādo hoti taṃ ca pajānāti, yathā ca uppannassa samādhisambojjhaṅgassa bhāvanāya pāripūrī hoti taṃ ca pajānāti.

When the factor of enlightenment, rapture,[22] is present in him, he understands properly, "The factor of enlightenment, rapture, is present in me." He understands properly that, when the factor of enlightenment, rapture, is absent from him, "The factor of enlightenment, rapture, is absent from me." He understands properly, how the factor of enlightenment, rapture, that has not yet arisen in him, comes to arise. He understands properly, how the factor of enlightenment, rapture, that has now arisen, is developed and perfected.

When the factor of enlightenment, tranquillity,[23] is present in him, he understands properly, "The factor of enlightenment, tranquillity, is present in me." He understands properly that, when the factor of enlightenment, tranquillity, is absent from him, "The factor of enlightenment, tranquillity is absent from me." He understands properly, how the factor of enlightenment, tranquillity, that has not yet arisen in him, comes to arise. He understands properly, how the factor of enlightenment, tranquillity, that has now arisen, is developed and perfected.

When the factor of enlightenment, concentration, is present in him, he understands properly, "The factor of enlightenment, concentration, is present in me." He understands properly that, when the factor of enlightenment, concentration, is absent from him, "The factor of enlightenment, concentration, is absent from me." He understands properly, how the factor of enlightenment, concentration, that has not yet arisen in him, comes to arise. He understands properly, how the factor of enlightenment, concentration, that has now arisen, is developed and perfected.

Santaṃ vā ajjhattaṃ upekkhāsambojjhaṅgaṃ 'atthi me ajjhattaṃ upekkhāsambojjhaṅgo' ti pajānāti, asantaṃ vā ajjhattaṃ upekkhāsambojjhaṅgaṃ 'natthi me ajjhattaṃ upekkhāsambojjhaṅgo' ti pajānāti, yathā ca anuppannassa upekkhāsambojjhaṅgassa uppādo hoti taṃ ca pajānāti, yathā ca uppannassa upekkhāsambojjhaṅgassa bhāvanāya pāripūrī hoti taṃ ca pajānāti.

Iti ajjhattaṃ vā dhammesu dhammānupassī viharati, bahiddhā vā dhammesu dhammānupassī viharati, ajjhattabahiddhā vā dhammesu dhammānupassī viharati, samudayadhammānupassī vā dhammesu viharati, vayadhammānupassī vā dhammesu viharati, samudayavaya-dhammānupassī vā dhammesu viharati, 'atthi dhammā' ti vā panassa sati paccupaṭṭhitā hoti. Yāvadeva ñāṇamattāya paṭissatimattāya anissito ca viharati, na ca kiñci loke upādiyati. Evaṃ pi kho, bhikkhave, bhikkhu dhammesu dhammānupassī viharati sattasu bojjhaṅgesu.

E. Saccapabbaṃ

Puna caparaṃ, bhikkhave, bhikkhu dhammesu dhammānupassī viharati catūsu ariyasaccesu.

Kathaṃ ca pana, bhikkhave, bhikkhu dhammesu dhammānupassī viharati catūsu ariyasaccesu?

Idha bhikkhave, bhikkhu 'idaṃ dukkhaṃ' ti yathābhūtaṃ pajānāti, 'ayaṃ dukkhasamudayo' ti yathābhūtaṃ pajānāti, 'ayaṃ dukkhanirodho' ti yathābhūtaṃ pajānāti, 'ayaṃ dukkhanirodhagāminī paṭipadā' ti yathābhūtaṃ pajānāti.

When the factor of enlightenment, equanimity, is present in him, he understands properly, "The factor of enlightenment, equanimity, is present in me." He understands properly that, when the factor of enlightenment, equanimity, is absent from him, "The factor of enlightenment, equanimity, is absent from me." He understands properly, how the factor of enlightenment, equanimity, that has not yet arisen in him, comes to arise. He understands properly, how the factor of enlightenment, equanimity, that has now arisen, is developed and perfected.

Thus he dwells observing mental contents in mental contents internally, or he dwells observing mental contents in mental contents externally, or he dwells observing mental contents in mental contents both internally and externally. Thus he dwells observing the phenomenon of arising in the mental contents, thus he dwells observing the phenomenon of passing away in the mental contents, thus he dwells observing the phenomenon of arising and passing away in the mental contents. Now his awareness is established: "These are mental contents!" Thus he develops his awareness to such an extent that there is mere understanding along with mere awareness. In this way he dwells detached, without clinging towards anything in the world [of mind and matter]. This is how, monks, a monk dwells observing mental contents in mental contents as regards the seven factors of enlightenment.

E. The Section on the Noble Truths

Again, monks, a monk dwells observing mental contents in mental contents, as regards the four noble truths.

How, monks, does a monk dwell observing mental contents in mental contents, as regards the four noble truths?

Here, monks, a monk understands properly as it is, "This is suffering"; he understands properly as it is, "This is the arising of suffering"; he understands properly as it is, "This is the cessation of suffering"; he understands properly as it is, "This is the path leading to the cessation of suffering."

Dukkhasaccaniddeso

Katamaṃ ca, bhikkhave, dukkhaṃ ariyasaccaṃ?

Jāti pi dukkhā, jarā pi dukkhā, (byādhi pi dukkhā,)[24] maraṇaṃ pi dukkhaṃ, sokaparidevadukkhadomanassupāyāsā pi dukkhā, appiyehi sampayogo pi dukkho, piyehi vippayogo pi dukkho, yampicchaṃ na labhati taṃ pi dukkhaṃ, saṅkhittena pañcupādānakkhandhā dukkhā.

Katamā ca, bhikkhave, jāti? Yā tesaṃ tesaṃ sattānaṃ tamhi tamhi sattanikāye jāti sañjāti okkanti abhinibbatti khandhānaṃ pātubhāvo āyatanānaṃ paṭilābho, ayaṃ vuccati, bhikkhave, jāti.

Katamā ca, bhikkhave, jarā? Yā tesaṃ tesaṃ sattānaṃ tamhi tamhi sattanikāye jarā jīraṇatā khaṇḍiccaṃ pāliccaṃ valittacatā āyuno saṃhāni indriyānaṃ paripāko, ayaṃ vuccati, bhikkhave, jarā.

Katamaṃ ca, bhikkhave, maraṇaṃ? Yaṃ tesaṃ tesaṃ sattānaṃ tamhā tamhā sattanikāyā cuti cavanatā bhedo antaradhānaṃ maccu maraṇaṃ kālakiriyā khandhānaṃ bhedo kaḷevarassa nikkhepo jīvitindriyassupacchedo, idaṃ vuccati, bhikkhave, maraṇaṃ.

Katamo ca, bhikkhave, soko? Yo kho, bhikkhave, aññataraññatarena byasanena samannāgatassa aññataraññatarena dukkhadhammena phuṭṭhassa soko socanā socitattaṃ antosoko antoparisoko, ayaṃ vuccati, bhikkhave, soko.

Exposition of the Truth of Suffering

And what, monks, is the Noble Truth of Suffering?

Birth is suffering, old age is suffering, (sickness is suffering),[24] death is suffering, sorrow, lamentation, pain, grief and distress are suffering, the association with something that one does not like is suffering, the disassociation with something that one does like is suffering, not to get what one desires is suffering; in short, the clinging to the five aggregates is suffering.

And what, monks, is birth? If there is birth for all kinds of beings in whatever kind of existence, their conception, their being born, their becoming, the coming into manifestation of their aggregates, the acquisition of their sense faculties—this, monks, is called birth.

And what, monks, is old age? If there is old age for all kinds of beings in whatever kind of existence, their getting frail and decrepit, the breaking [of their teeth], their becoming grey and wrinkled, the running down of their life span, the deterioration of their sense faculties—this, monks, is called old age.

And what, monks, is death? If there is vanishing and passing away for all kinds of beings in whatever kind of existence, their disintegration, their disappearance, their dying, their death, the completion of their life span, the dissolution of the aggregates, the discarding of the body, the destruction of their vitality—this, monks, is called death.

And what, monks, is sorrow? Whenever one, monks, is affected by various kinds of loss and misfortune, that are followed by this or that kind of painful state of mind, by sorrow, by mourning, by sorrowfulness, by inward grief, and by deep inward woe—this, monks, is called sorrow.

Katamo ca, bhikkhave, paridevo? Yo kho, bhikkhave, aññataraññatarena byasanena samannāgatassa aññataraññatarena dukkhadhammena phuṭṭhassa ādevo paridevo ādevanā paridevanā ādevitattaṃ paridevitattaṃ, ayaṃ vuccati, bhikkhave, paridevo.

Katamaṃ ca, bhikkhave, dukkhaṃ?[25] Yaṃ kho, bhikkhave, kāyikaṃ dukkhaṃ kāyikaṃ asātaṃ kāyasamphassajaṃ dukkhaṃ asātaṃ vedayitaṃ, idaṃ vuccati, bhikkhave, dukkhaṃ.

Katamaṃ ca, bhikkhave, domanassaṃ?[25] Yaṃ kho, bhikkhave, cetasikaṃ dukkhaṃ cetasikaṃ asātaṃ manosamphassajaṃ dukkhaṃ asātaṃ vedayitaṃ, idaṃ vuccati, bhikkhave, domanassaṃ.

Katamo ca, bhikkhave, upāyāso? Yo kho, bhikkhave, aññataraññatarena byasanena samannāgatassa aññataraññatarena dukkhadhammena phuṭṭhassa āyāso upāyāso āyāsitattaṃ upāyāsitattaṃ, ayaṃ vuccati, bhikkhave, upāyāso.

Katamo ca, bhikkhave, appiyehi sampayogo dukkho? Idha yassa te honti aniṭṭhā akantā amanāpā rūpā saddā gandhā rasā phoṭṭhabbā dhammā, ye vā panassa te honti anatthakāmā ahitakāmā aphāsukakāmā ayogakkhemakāmā, yā tehi saddhiṃ saṅgati samāgamo samodhānaṃ missībhāvo, ayaṃ vuccati, bhikkhave, appiyehi sampayogo dukkho.

And what, monks, is lamentation? Whenever one, monks, is affected by various kinds of loss and misfortune, that are followed by this or that kind of painful state of mind, by wailing and crying, by lamentation, by deep wailing, by deep lamentation, by the state of deep wailing and deep lamentation—this, monks, is called lamentation.

And what, monks, is pain?[25] If there is, monks, any kind of bodily pain, any kind of bodily unpleasantness or any kind of painful or unpleasant sensation as a result of bodily contact—this, monks, is called pain.

And what, monks, is grief?[25] If there is, monks, any kind of mental pain, any kind of mental unpleasantness or any kind of painful or unpleasant sensation as a result of mental contact—this, monks, is called grief.

And what, monks, is distress? Whenever one, monks, is affected by various kinds of loss and misfortune, that are followed by this or that kind of painful state of mind, by tribulation, by distress, affliction with distress and affliction with great distress—this, monks, is called distress.

And what, monks, is the suffering of being associated with what one does not like? Wherever and whenever one finds unpleasant, disagreeable or disliked objects of sight, sound, smell, taste, touch or of the mind, or, whenever and wherever one finds that there are wishers of one's own misfortune, harm, difficulties or of one's own insecurity; if one gets associated, one meets, one comes into contact or gets combined with them—this, monks, is called the suffering of being associated with what one does not like.

Katamo ca, bhikkhave, piyehi vippayogo dukkho? Idha yassa te honti iṭṭhā kantā manāpā rūpā saddā gandhā rasā phoṭṭhabbā dhammā, ye vā panassa te honti atthakāmā hitakāmā phāsukakāmā yogakkhemakāmā mātā vā pitā vā bhātā vā bhaginī vā mittā vā amaccā vā ñātisālohitā vā, yā tehi saddhiṃ asaṅgati asamāgamo asamodhānaṃ amissībhāvo, ayaṃ vuccati, bhikkhave, piyehi vippayogo dukkho.

Katamaṃ ca, bhikkhave, yampicchaṃ na labhati taṃ pi dukkhaṃ? Jātidhammānaṃ, bhikkhave, sattānaṃ evaṃ icchā uppajjati: 'aho vata mayaṃ na jātidhammā assāma na ca vata no jāti āgaccheyyā' ti. Na kho panetaṃ icchāya pattabbaṃ. Idaṃ pi yampicchaṃ na labhati taṃ pi dukkhaṃ.

Jarādhammānaṃ, bhikkhave, sattānaṃ evaṃ icchā uppajjati: 'aho vata mayaṃ na jarādhammā assāma, na ca vata no jarā āgaccheyyā' ti. Na kho panetaṃ icchāya pattabbaṃ. Idaṃ pi yampicchaṃ na labhati taṃ pi dukkhaṃ.

Byādhidhammānaṃ, bhikkhave, sattānaṃ evaṃ icchā uppajjati: 'aho vata mayaṃ na byādhidhammā assāma, na ca vata no byādhi āgaccheyyā' ti. Na kho panetaṃ icchāya pattabbaṃ. Idaṃ pi yampicchaṃ na labhati taṃ pi dukkhaṃ.

Maraṇadhammānaṃ, bhikkhave, sattānaṃ evaṃ icchā uppajjati: 'aho vata mayaṃ na maraṇadhammā assāma, na ca vata no maraṇaṃ āgaccheyyā' ti. Na kho panetaṃ icchāya pattabbaṃ. Idaṃ pi yampicchaṃ na labhati taṃ pi dukkhaṃ.

And what, monks, is the suffering of being disassociated with what one does like? Wherever and whenever one finds pleasant, agreeable or liked objects of sight, sound, smell, taste, touch or of the mind, or, whenever and wherever one finds that there are wishers of one's own fortune, prosperity, comfort or of one's own security, like mother and father, like brother and sister, like friends and colleagues or relatives; if one gets disassociated, one does not meet, one does not come into contact or does not get combined with them—this, monks, is called the suffering of being disassociated with what one does like.

And what, monks, is not getting what one desires? In beings, monks, who are subject to birth the desire arises: "Oh, truly, that we were not subject to birth! Oh, truly, may there be no new birth for us!" But this cannot be obtained by mere desire; and not to get what one wants is suffering.

In beings, monks, who are subject to old age the desire arises: "Oh, truly, that we were not subject to old age! Oh, truly, may we not be subject to old age!" But this cannot be obtained by mere desire; and not to get what one wants is suffering.

In beings, monks, who are subject to sickness the desire arises: "Oh, truly, that we were not subject to sickness! Oh, truly, may there be no sickness for us!" But this cannot be obtained by mere desire; and not to get what one wants is suffering.

In beings, monks, who are subject to death the desire arises: "Oh, truly, that we were not subject to death! Oh, truly, may we never have to die!" But this cannot be obtained by mere desire; and not to get what one wants is suffering.

Sokaparidevadukkhadomanassupāyāsadhammānaṃ, bhikkhave, sattānaṃ evaṃ icchā uppajjati: 'aho vata mayaṃ na sokaparidevadukkhadomanassupāyāsadhammā assāma, na ca vata no sokaparidevadukkhadomanassupāyāsadhammā āgaccheyyuṃ' ti. Na kho panetaṃ icchāya pattabbaṃ. Idaṃ pi yampicchaṃ na labhati taṃ pi dukkhaṃ.

Katame ca, bhikkhave, saṅkhittena pañcupādānakkhandhā dukkhā? Seyyathidaṃ—rūpupādānakkhandho vedanupādānakkhandho saññupādānakkhandho saṅkhārupādānakkhandho viññāṇupādānakkhandho. Ime vuccanti, bhikkhave, saṅkhittena pañcupādānakkhandhā dukkhā.

Idaṃ vuccati, bhikkhave, dukkhaṃ ariyasaccaṃ.

Samudayasaccaniddeso

Katamaṃ ca, bhikkhave, dukkhasamudayaṃ ariyasaccaṃ?

Yāyaṃ taṇhā ponobbhavikā nandīrāgasahagatā tatratatrābhinandinī, seyyathidaṃ, kāmataṇhā bhavataṇhā vibhavataṇhā.

Sā kho panesā, bhikkhave, taṇhā kattha uppajjamānā uppajjati, kattha nivisamānā nivisati?

Yaṃ loke piyarūpaṃ sātarūpaṃ etthesā taṇhā uppajjamānā uppajjati, ettha nivisamānā nivisati.

In beings, monks, who are subject to sorrow, lamentation, pain, grief and distress the desire arises: "Oh, truly, that we were not subject to sorrow, lamentation, pain, grief and distress! Oh, truly, may we not suffer from sorrow, lamentation, pain, grief and distress!" But this cannot be obtained by mere desire; and not to get what one wants is suffering.

And how, monks, in short, is clinging to the five aggregates suffering? It is as follows—clinging to the aggregate of matter is suffering, clinging to the aggregate of sensation is suffering, clinging to the aggregate of perception is suffering, clinging to the aggregate of reaction is suffering, clinging to the aggregate of consciousness is suffering. This, monks, in short, is called suffering because of clinging to these five aggregates.

This, monks, is the Noble Truth of Suffering.

Exposition of the Truth of the Arising of Suffering

And what, monks, is the Noble Truth of the Arising of Suffering?

It is this craving that occurs again and again and is bound up with pleasure and lust and finds delight now here, now there. That is, the craving for sensual pleasures, the craving for repeated rebirth and the craving for annihilation.

But where does this craving, monks, arise and where does it get established?

Wherever in the world [of mind and matter] there is something enticing and pleasurable, there this craving arises and gets established.

Kiñca loke[26] piyarūpaṃ sātarūpaṃ? Cakkhu loke piyarūpaṃ sātarūpaṃ, etthesā taṇhā uppajjamānā uppajjati, ettha nivisamānā nivisati. Sotaṃ loke piyarūpaṃ sātarūpaṃ, etthesā taṇhā uppajjamānā uppajjati, ettha nivisamānā nivisati. Ghānaṃ loke piyarūpaṃ sātarūpaṃ, etthesā taṇhā uppajjamānā uppajjati, ettha nivisamānā nivisati. Jivhā loke piyarūpaṃ sātarūpaṃ, etthesā taṇhā uppajjamānā uppajjati, ettha nivisamānā nivisati. Kāyo loke piyarūpaṃ sātarūpaṃ, etthesā taṇhā uppajjamānā uppajjati, ettha nivisamānā nivisati. Mano loke piyarūpaṃ sātarūpaṃ, etthesā taṇhā uppajjamānā uppajjati, ettha nivisamānā nivisati.

Rūpā loke piyarūpaṃ sātarūpaṃ, etthesā taṇhā uppajjamānā uppajjati, ettha nivisamānā nivisati. Saddā loke piyarūpaṃ sātarūpaṃ, etthesā taṇhā uppajjamānā uppajjati, ettha nivisamānā nivisati. Gandhā loke piyarūpaṃ sātarūpaṃ, etthesā taṇhā uppajjamānā uppajjati, ettha nivisamānā nivisati. Rasā loke piyarūpaṃ sātarūpaṃ, etthesā taṇhā uppajjamānā uppajjati, ettha nivisamānā nivisati. Phoṭṭhabbā loke piyarūpaṃ sātarūpaṃ, etthesā taṇhā uppajjamānā uppajjati, ettha nivisamānā nivisati. Dhammā loke piyarūpaṃ sātarūpaṃ, etthesā taṇhā uppajjamānā uppajjati, ettha nivisamānā nivisati.

Cakkhuviññāṇaṃ loke piyarūpaṃ sātarūpaṃ, etthesā taṇhā uppajjamānā uppajjati, ettha nivisamānā nivisati. Sotaviññāṇaṃ loke piyarūpaṃ sātarūpaṃ, etthesā taṇhā uppajjamānā uppajjati, ettha nivisamānā nivisati. Ghānaviññāṇaṃ loke piyarūpaṃ sātarūpaṃ, etthesā taṇhā uppajjamānā uppajjati, ettha nivisamānā nivisati. Jivhāviññāṇaṃ loke piyarūpaṃ sātarūpaṃ, etthesā taṇhā uppajjamānā uppajjati, ettha nivisamānā nivisati. Kāyaviññāṇaṃ loke piyarūpaṃ sātarūpaṃ, etthesā taṇhā uppajjamānā uppajjati, ettha nivisamānā nivisati. Manoviññāṇaṃ loke piyarūpaṃ sātarūpaṃ, etthesā taṇhā uppajjamānā uppajjati, ettha nivisamānā nivisati.

But what in the world[26] [of mind and matter] is enticing and pleasurable? The eye in the world [of mind and matter] is enticing and pleasurable; there this craving arises and gets established. The ear … is enticing and pleasurable; there this craving arises and gets established. The nose … is enticing and pleasurable; there this craving arises and gets established. The tongue … is enticing and pleasurable; there this craving arises and gets established. The body … is enticing and pleasurable; there this craving arises and gets established. The mind in the world [of mind and matter] is enticing and pleasurable; there this craving arises and gets established.

Visible objects, material forms in the world [of mind and matter], are enticing and pleasurable; there this craving arises and gets established. Sounds … are enticing and pleasurable; there this craving arises and gets established. Smells … are enticing and pleasurable; there this craving arises and gets established. Tastes … are enticing and pleasurable; there this craving arises and gets established. Touch … is enticing and pleasurable; there this craving arises and gets established. The contents of the mind in the world [of mind and matter] are enticing and pleasurable; there this craving arises and gets established.

The eye consciousness in the world [of mind and matter] is enticing and pleasurable; there this craving arises and gets established. The ear consciousness … is enticing and pleasurable; there this craving arises and gets established. The nose consciousness … is enticing and pleasurable; there this craving arises and gets established. The tongue consciousness … is enticing and pleasurable; there this craving arises and gets established. The body consciousness … is enticing and pleasurable; there this craving arises and gets established. The mind consciousness in the world [of mind and matter] is enticing and pleasurable; there this craving arises and gets established.

Cakkhusamphasso loke piyarūpaṃ sātarūpaṃ, etthesā taṇhā uppajjamānā uppajjati, ettha nivisamānā nivisati. Sotasamphasso loke piyarūpaṃ sātarūpaṃ, etthesā taṇhā uppajjamānā uppajjati, ettha nivisamānā nivisati. Ghānasamphasso loke piyarūpaṃ sātarūpaṃ, etthesā taṇhā uppajjamānā uppajjati, ettha nivisamānā nivisati. Jivhāsamphasso loke piyarūpaṃ sātarūpaṃ, etthesā taṇhā uppajjamānā uppajjati, ettha nivisamānā nivisati. Kāyasamphasso loke piyarūpaṃ sātarūpaṃ, etthesā taṇhā uppajjamānā uppajjati, ettha nivisamānā nivisati. Manosamphasso loke piyarūpaṃ sātarūpaṃ, etthesā taṇhā uppajjamānā uppajjati, ettha nivisamānā nivisati.

Cakkhusamphassajā vedanā loke piyarūpaṃ sātarūpaṃ, etthesā taṇhā uppajjamānā uppajjati, ettha nivisamānā nivisati. Sotasamphassajā vedanā loke piyarūpaṃ sātarūpaṃ, etthesā taṇhā uppajjamānā uppajjati, ettha nivisamānā nivisati. Ghānasamphassajā vedanā loke piyarūpaṃ sātarūpaṃ, etthesā taṇhā uppajjamānā uppajjati, ettha nivisamānā nivisati. Jivhāsamphassajā vedanā loke piyarūpaṃ sātarūpaṃ, etthesā taṇhā uppajjamānā uppajjati, ettha nivisamānā nivisati. Kāyasamphassajā vedanā loke piyarūpaṃ sātarūpaṃ, etthesā taṇhā uppajjamānā uppajjati, ettha nivisamānā nivisati. Manosamphassajā vedanā loke piyarūpaṃ sātarūpaṃ, etthesā taṇhā uppajjamānā uppajjati, ettha nivisamānā nivisati.

Rūpasaññā loke piyarūpaṃ sātarūpaṃ, etthesā taṇhā uppajjamānā uppajjati, ettha nivisamānā nivisati. Saddasaññā loke piyarūpaṃ sātarūpaṃ, etthesā taṇhā uppajjamānā uppajjati, ettha nivisamānā nivisati. Gandhasaññā loke piyarūpaṃ sātarūpaṃ, etthesā taṇhā uppajjamānā uppajjati, ettha nivisamānā nivisati. Rasasaññā loke piyarūpaṃ sātarūpaṃ, etthesā taṇhā uppajjamānā uppajjati, ettha nivisamānā nivisati. Phoṭṭhabbasaññā loke piyarūpaṃ sātarūpaṃ, etthesā taṇhā uppajjamānā uppajjati, ettha nivisamānā nivisati. Dhammasaññā loke piyarūpaṃ sātarūpaṃ, etthesā taṇhā uppajjamānā uppajjati, ettha nivisamānā nivisati.

The eye contact in the world [of mind and matter] is enticing and pleasurable; there this craving arises and gets established. The ear-contact ... is enticing and pleasurable; there this craving arises and gets established. The nose-contact ... is enticing and pleasurable; there this craving arises and gets established. The tongue-contact ... is enticing and pleasurable; there this craving arises and gets established. The body-contact ... is enticing and pleasurable; there this craving arises and gets established. The mind-contact in the world [of mind and matter] is enticing and pleasurable; there this craving arises and gets established.

The sensation arising from the eye-contact in the world [of mind and matter] is enticing and pleasurable; there this craving arises and gets established. The sensation arising from the ear-contact ... is enticing and pleasurable; there this craving arises and gets established. The sensation arising from the nose-contact ... is enticing and pleasurable; there this craving arises and gets established. The sensation arising from the tongue-contact ... is enticing and pleasurable; there this craving arises and gets established. The sensation arising from the body-contact ... is enticing and pleasurable; there this craving arises and gets established. The sensation arising from the mind-contact in the world [of mind and matter] is enticing and pleasurable; there this craving arises and gets established.

The perception of visible objects, of material forms, in the world [of mind and matter] is enticing and pleasurable; there this craving arises and gets established. The perception of sounds ... is enticing and pleasurable; there this craving arises and gets established. The perception of smells ... is enticing and pleasurable; there this craving arises and gets established. The perception of tastes ... is enticing and pleasurable; there this craving arises and gets established. The perception of touch ... is enticing and pleasurable; there this craving arises and gets established. The perception of mental contents in the world [of mind and matter] is enticing and pleasurable; there this craving arises and gets established.

Rūpasañcetanā loke piyarūpaṃ sātarūpaṃ, etthesā taṇhā uppajjamānā uppajjati, ettha nivisamānā nivisati. Saddasañcetanā loke piyarūpaṃ sātarūpaṃ, etthesā taṇhā uppajjamānā uppajjati, ettha nivisamānā nivisati. Gandhasañcetanā loke piyarūpaṃ sātarūpaṃ, etthesā taṇhā uppajjamānā uppajjati, ettha nivisamānā nivisati. Rasasañcetanā loke piyarūpaṃ sātarūpaṃ, etthesā taṇhā uppajjamānā uppajjati, ettha nivisamānā nivisati. Phoṭṭhabbasañcetanā loke piyarūpaṃ sātarūpaṃ, etthesā taṇhā uppajjamānā uppajjati, ettha nivisamānā nivisati. Dhammasañcetanā loke piyarūpaṃ sātarūpaṃ, etthesā taṇhā uppajjamānā uppajjati, ettha nivisamānā nivisati.

Rūpataṇhā loke piyarūpaṃ sātarūpaṃ, etthesā taṇhā uppajjamānā uppajjati, ettha nivisamānā nivisati. Saddataṇhā loke piyarūpaṃ sātarūpaṃ, etthesā taṇhā uppajjamānā uppajjati, ettha nivisamānā nivisati. Gandhataṇhā loke piyarūpaṃ sātarūpaṃ, etthesā taṇhā uppajjamānā uppajjati, ettha nivisamānā nivisati. Rasataṇhā loke piyarūpaṃ sātarūpaṃ, etthesā taṇhā uppajjamānā uppajjati, ettha nivisamānā nivisati. Phoṭṭhabbataṇhā loke piyarūpaṃ sātarūpaṃ, etthesā taṇhā uppajjamānā uppajjati, ettha nivisamānā nivisati. Dhammataṇhā loke piyarūpaṃ sātarūpaṃ, etthesā taṇhā uppajjamānā uppajjati, ettha nivisamānā nivisati.

Rūpavitakko[27] loke piyarūpaṃ sātarūpaṃ, etthesā taṇhā uppajjamānā uppajjati, ettha nivisamānā nivisati. Saddavitakko loke piyarūpaṃ sātarūpaṃ, etthesā taṇhā uppajjamānā uppajjati, ettha nivisamānā nivisati. Gandhavitakko loke piyarūpaṃ sātarūpaṃ, etthesā taṇhā uppajjamānā uppajjati, ettha nivisamānā nivisati. Rasavitakko loke piyarūpaṃ sātarūpaṃ, etthesā taṇhā uppajjamānā uppajjati, ettha nivisamānā nivisati. Phoṭṭhabbavitakko loke piyarūpaṃ sātarūpaṃ, etthesā taṇhā uppajjamānā uppajjati, ettha nivisamānā nivisati. Dhammavitakko loke piyarūpaṃ sātarūpaṃ, etthesā taṇhā uppajjamānā uppajjati, ettha nivisamānā nivisati.

The mental reaction to visible objects in the world [of mind and matter] is enticing and pleasurable; there this craving arises and gets established. The mental reaction to sounds ... is enticing and pleasurable; there this craving arises and gets established. The mental reaction to smells ... is enticing and pleasurable; there this craving arises and gets established. The mental reaction to tastes ... is enticing and pleasurable; there this craving arises and gets established. The mental reaction to touch ... is enticing and pleasurable; there this craving arises and gets established. The mental reaction to mind objects, mental contents in the world [of mind and matter] is enticing and pleasurable; there this craving arises and gets established.

The craving after visible objects in the world [of mind and matter] is enticing and pleasurable; there this craving arises and gets established. The craving after sounds ... is enticing and pleasurable; there this craving arises and gets established. The craving after smells ... is enticing and pleasurable; there this craving arises and gets established. The craving after tastes ... is enticing and pleasurable; there this craving arises and gets established. The craving after touch ... is enticing and pleasurable; there this craving arises and gets established. The craving after mind objects, mental contents in the world [of mind and matter] is enticing and pleasurable; there this craving arises and gets established.

The thought conception[27] of visible objects in the world [of mind and matter] is enticing and pleasurable; there this craving arises and gets established. The thought conception of sounds ... is enticing and pleasurable; there this craving arises and gets established. The thought conception of smells ... is enticing and pleasurable; there this craving arises and gets established. The thought conception of tastes ... is enticing and pleasurable; there this craving arises and gets established. The thought conception of touch ... is enticing and pleasurable; there this craving arises and gets established. The thought conception of mind objects, mental contents in the world [of mind and matter] is enticing and pleasurable; there this craving arises and gets established.

Rūpavicāro loke piyarūpaṃ sātarūpaṃ, etthesā taṇhā uppajjamānā uppajjati, ettha nivisamānā nivisati. Saddavicāro loke piyarūpaṃ sātarūpaṃ, etthesā taṇhā uppajjamānā uppajjati, ettha nivisamānā nivisati. Gandhavicāro loke piyarūpaṃ sātarūpaṃ, etthesā taṇhā uppajjamānā uppajjati, ettha nivisamānā nivisati. Rasavicāro loke piyarūpaṃ sātarūpaṃ, etthesā taṇhā uppajjamānā uppajjati, ettha nivisamānā nivisati. Phoṭṭhabbavicāro loke piyarūpaṃ sātarūpaṃ, etthesā taṇhā uppajjamānā uppajjati, ettha nivisamānā nivisati. Dhammavicāro loke piyarūpaṃ sātarūpaṃ, etthesā taṇhā uppajjamānā uppajjati, ettha nivisamānā nivisati.

Idaṃ vuccati, bhikkhave, dukkhasamudayaṃ ariyasaccaṃ.

Nirodhasaccaniddeso

Katamaṃ ca, bhikkhave, dukkhanirodhaṃ ariyasaccaṃ?

Yo tassāyeva taṇhāya asesavirāganirodho cāgo paṭinissaggo mutti anālayo. Sā kho panesā, bhikkhave, taṇhā kattha pahīyamānā pahīyati, kattha nirujjhamānā nirujjhati? Yaṃ loke piyarūpaṃ sātarūpaṃ, etthesā taṇhā pahīyamānā pahīyati, ettha nirujjhamānā nirujjhati.

The rolling in thoughts of visible objects in the world [of mind and matter] is enticing and pleasurable; there this craving arises and gets established. The rolling in thoughts of sounds … is enticing and pleasurable; there this craving arises and gets established. The rolling in thoughts of smells … is enticing and pleasurable; there this craving arises and gets established. The rolling in thoughts of tastes … is enticing and pleasurable; there this craving arises and gets established. The rolling in thoughts of touch … is enticing and pleasurable; there this craving arises and gets established. The rolling in thoughts of mind objects, mental contents in the world [of mind and matter] is enticing and pleasurable; there this craving arises and gets established.

This, monks, is the Noble Truth of the Arising of Suffering.

Exposition of the Truth of the Cessation of Suffering

And what, monks, is the Noble Truth of the Cessation of Suffering?

It is the complete fading away and cessation of this very craving, forsaking it and giving it up; the liberation from it, leaving no place for it. But where may this craving, monks, be eradicated; where may it be extinguished? Wherever in the world [of mind and matter] there is something enticing and pleasurable: there this craving may be eradicated and extinguished.

Kiñca loke piyarūpaṃ sātarūpaṃ? Cakkhu loke piyarūpaṃ sātarūpaṃ, etthesā taṇhā pahīyamānā pahīyati, ettha nirujjhamānā nirujjhati. Sotaṃ loke piyarūpaṃ sātarūpaṃ, etthesā taṇhā pahīyamānā pahīyati, ettha nirujjhamānā nirujjhati. Ghānaṃ loke piyarūpaṃ sātarūpaṃ, etthesā taṇhā pahīyamānā pahīyati, ettha nirujjhamānā nirujjhati. Jivhā loke piyarūpaṃ sātarūpaṃ, etthesā taṇhā pahīyamānā pahīyati, ettha nirujjhamānā nirujjhati. Kāyo loke piyarūpaṃ sātarūpaṃ, etthesā taṇhā pahīyamānā pahīyati, ettha nirujjhamānā nirujjhati. Mano loke piyarūpaṃ sātarūpaṃ, etthesā taṇhā pahīyamānā pahīyati, ettha nirujjhamānā nirujjhati.

Rūpā loke piyarūpaṃ sātarūpaṃ, etthesā taṇhā pahīyamānā pahīyati, ettha nirujjhamānā nirujjhati. Saddā loke piyarūpaṃ sātarūpaṃ, etthesā taṇhā pahīyamānā pahīyati, ettha nirujjhamānā nirujjhati. Gandhā loke piyarūpaṃ sātarūpaṃ, etthesā taṇhā pahīyamānā pahīyati, ettha nirujjhamānā nirujjhati. Rasā loke piyarūpaṃ sātarūpaṃ, etthesā taṇhā pahīyamānā pahīyati, ettha nirujjhamānā nirujjhati. Phoṭṭhabbā loke piyarūpaṃ sātarūpaṃ, etthesā taṇhā pahīyamānā pahīyati, ettha nirujjhamānā nirujjhati. Dhammā loke piyarūpaṃ sātarūpaṃ, etthesā taṇhā pahīyamānā pahīyati, ettha nirujjhamānā nirujjhati.

Cakkhuviññāṇaṃ loke piyarūpaṃ sātarūpaṃ, etthesā taṇhā pahīyamānā pahīyati, ettha nirujjhamānā nirujjhati. Sotaviññāṇaṃ loke piyarūpaṃ sātarūpaṃ, etthesā taṇhā pahīyamānā pahīyati, ettha nirujjhamānā nirujjhati. Ghānaviññāṇaṃ loke piyarūpaṃ sātarūpaṃ, etthesā taṇhā pahīyamānā pahīyati, ettha nirujjhamānā nirujjhati. Jivhāviññāṇaṃ loke piyarūpaṃ sātarūpaṃ, etthesā taṇhā pahīyamānā pahīyati, ettha nirujjhamānā nirujjhati. Kāyaviññāṇaṃ loke piyarūpaṃ sātarūpaṃ, etthesā taṇhā pahīyamāna pahīyati, ettha nirujjhamānā nirujjhati. Manoviññāṇaṃ loke piyarūpaṃ sātarūpaṃ, etthesā taṇhā pahīyamānā pahīyati, ettha nirujjhamānā nirujjhati.

But what in the world [of mind and matter] is enticing and pleasurable? The eye in the world [of mind and matter] is enticing and pleasurable; there this craving may be eradicated and extinguished. The ear … is enticing and pleasurable; there this craving may be eradicated and extinguished. The nose … is enticing and pleasurable; there this craving may be eradicated and extinguished. The tongue … is enticing and pleasurable; there this craving may be eradicated and extinguished. The body … is enticing and pleasurable; there this craving may be eradicated and extinguished. The mind in the world [of mind and matter] is enticing and pleasurable; there this craving may be eradicated and extinguished.

The objects of sight, the material forms in the world [of mind and matter], are enticing and pleasurable; there this craving may be eradicated and extinguished. The sounds … are enticing and pleasurable; there this craving may be eradicated and extinguished. The smells … are enticing and pleasurable; there this craving may be eradicated and extinguished. The tastes … are enticing and pleasurable; there this craving may be eradicated and extinguished. Touch … is enticing and pleasurable; there this craving may be eradicated and extinguished. The contents of the mind in the world [of mind and matter] are enticing and pleasurable; there this craving may be eradicated and extinguished.

The eye-consciousness in the world [of mind and matter] is enticing and pleasurable; there this craving may be eradicated and extinguished. The ear-consciousness … is enticing and pleasurable; there this craving may be eradicated and extinguished. The nose-consciousness … is enticing and pleasurable; there this craving may be eradicated and extinguished. The tongue-consciousness … is enticing and pleasurable; there this craving may be eradicated and extinguished. The body-consciousness … is enticing and pleasurable; there this craving may be eradicated and extinguished. The mind-consciousness in the world [of mind and matter] is enticing and pleasurable; there this craving may be eradicated and extinguished.

Cakkhusamphasso loke piyarūpaṃ sātarūpaṃ, etthesā taṇhā pahīyamānā pahīyati, ettha nirujjhamānā nirujjhati. Sotasamphasso loke piyarūpaṃ sātarūpaṃ, etthesā taṇhā pahīyamānā pahīyati, ettha nirujjhamānā nirujjhati. Ghānasamphasso loke piyarūpaṃ sātarūpaṃ, etthesā taṇhā pahīyamānā pahīyati, ettha nirujjhamānā nirujjhati. Jivhāsamphasso loke piyarūpaṃ sātarūpaṃ, etthesā taṇhā pahīyamānā pahīyati, ettha nirujjhamānā nirujjhati. Kāyasamphasso loke piyarūpaṃ sātarūpaṃ, etthesā taṇhā pahīyamānā pahīyati, ettha nirujjhamānā nirujjhati. Manosamphasso loke piyarūpaṃ sātarūpaṃ, etthesā taṇhā pahīyamānā pahīyati, ettha nirujjhamānā nirujjhati.

Cakkhusamphassajā vedanā loke piyarūpaṃ sātarūpaṃ, etthesā taṇhā pahīyamānā pahīyati, ettha nirujjhamānā nirujjhati. Sotasamphassajā vedanā loke piyarūpaṃ sātarūpaṃ, etthesā taṇhā pahīyamānā pahīyati, ettha nirujjhamānā nirujjhati. Ghānasamphassajā vedanā loke piyarūpaṃ sātarūpaṃ, etthesā taṇhā pahīyamānā pahīyati, ettha nirujjhamānā nirujjhati. Jivhāsamphassajā vedanā loke piyarūpaṃ sātarūpaṃ, etthesā taṇhā pahīyamānā pahīyati, ettha nirujjhamānā nirujjhati. Kāyasamphassajā vedanā loke piyarūpaṃ sātarūpaṃ, etthesā taṇhā pahīyamānā pahīyati, ettha nirujjhamānā nirujjhati. Manosamphassajā vedanā loke piyarūpaṃ sātarūpaṃ, etthesā taṇhā pahīyamānā pahīyati, ettha nirujjhamānā nirujjhati.

The eye-contact in the world [of mind and matter] is enticing and pleasurable; there this craving may be eradicated and extinguished. The ear-contact ... is enticing and pleasurable; there this craving may be eradicated and extinguished. The nose-contact ... is enticing and pleasurable; there this craving may be eradicated and extinguished. The tongue-contact ... is enticing and pleasurable; there this craving may be eradicated and extinguished. The body-contact ... is enticing and pleasurable; there this craving may be eradicated and extinguished. The mind-contact in the world [of mind and matter] is enticing and pleasurable; there this craving may be eradicated and extinguished.

The sensation that arises from the eye contact in the world [of mind and matter] is enticing and pleasurable; there this craving may be eradicated and extinguished. The sensation that arises from the ear contact ... is enticing and pleasurable; there this craving may be eradicated and extinguished. The sensation that arises from the nose contact ... is enticing and pleasurable; there this craving may be eradicated and extinguished. The sensation that arises from the tongue contact ... is enticing and pleasurable; there this craving may be eradicated and extinguished. The sensation that arises from the body contact ... is enticing and pleasurable; there this craving may be eradicated and extinguished. The sensation that arises from the mind contact in the world [of mind and matter] is enticing and pleasurable; there this craving may be eradicated and extinguished.

Rūpasaññā loke piyarūpaṃ sātarūpaṃ, etthesā taṇhā pahīyamānā pahīyati, ettha nirujjhamānā nirujjhati. Saddasaññā loke piyarūpaṃ sātarūpaṃ, etthesā taṇhā pahīyamānā pahīyati, ettha nirujjhamānā nirujjhati. Gandhasaññā loke piyarūpaṃ sātarūpaṃ, etthesā taṇhā pahīyamānā pahīyati, ettha nirujjhamānā nirujjhati. Rasasaññā loke piyarūpaṃ sātarūpaṃ, etthesā taṇhā pahīyamānā pahīyati, ettha nirujjhamānā nirujjhati. Phoṭṭhabbasaññā loke piyarūpaṃ sātarūpaṃ, etthesā taṇhā pahīyamānā pahīyati, ettha nirujjhamānā nirujjhati. Dhammasaññā loke piyarūpaṃ sātarūpaṃ, etthesā taṇhā pahīyamānā pahīyati, ettha nirujjhamānā nirujjhati.

Rūpasañcetanā loke piyarūpaṃ sātarūpaṃ, etthesā taṇhā pahīyamānā pahīyati, ettha nirujjhamānā nirujjhati. Saddasañcetanā loke piyarūpaṃ sātarūpaṃ, etthesā taṇhā pahīyamānā pahīyati, ettha nirujjhamānā nirujjhati. Gandhasañcetanā loke piyarūpaṃ sātarūpaṃ, etthesā taṇhā pahīyamānā pahīyati, ettha nirujjhamānā nirujjhati. Rasasañcetanā loke piyarūpaṃ sātarūpaṃ, etthesā taṇhā pahīyamānā pahīyati, ettha nirujjhamānā nirujjhati. Phoṭṭhabbasañcetanā loke piyarūpaṃ sātarūpaṃ, etthesā taṇhā pahīyamānā pahīyati, ettha nirujjhamānā nirujjhati. Dhammasañcetanā loke piyarūpaṃ sātarūpaṃ, etthesā taṇhā pahīyamānā pahīyati, ettha nirujjhamānā nirujjhati.

The perception of visible objects in the world [of mind and matter] is enticing and pleasurable; there this craving may be eradicated and extinguished. The perception of sounds … is enticing and pleasurable; there this craving may be eradicated and extinguished. The perception of smells … is enticing and pleasurable; there this craving may be eradicated and extinguished. The perception of tastes … is enticing and pleasurable; there this craving may be eradicated and extinguished. The perception of touch … is enticing and pleasurable; there this craving may be eradicated and extinguished. The perception of mental contents in the world [of mind and matter] is enticing and pleasurable; there this craving may be eradicated and extinguished.

The mental reaction towards visible objects in the world [of mind and matter] is enticing and pleasurable; there this craving may be eradicated and extinguished. The mental reaction towards sounds … is enticing and pleasurable; there this craving may be eradicated and extinguished. The mental reaction towards smells … is enticing and pleasurable; there this craving may be eradicated and extinguished. The mental reaction towards tastes … is enticing and pleasurable; there this craving may be eradicated and extinguished. The mental reaction towards touch … is enticing and pleasurable; there this craving may be eradicated and extinguished. The mental reaction towards mental contents in the world [of mind and matter] is enticing and pleasurable; there this craving may be eradicated and extinguished.

Rūpataṇhā loke piyarūpaṃ sātarūpaṃ, etthesā taṇhā pahīyamānā pahīyati, ettha nirujjhamānā nirujjhati. Saddataṇhā loke piyarūpaṃ sātarūpaṃ, etthesā taṇhā pahīyamānā pahīyati, ettha nirujjhamānā nirujjhati. Gandhataṇhā loke piyarūpaṃ sātarūpaṃ, etthesā taṇhā pahīyamānā pahīyati, ettha nirujjhamānā nirujjhati. Rasataṇhā loke piyarūpaṃ sātarūpaṃ, etthesā taṇhā pahīyamānā pahīyati, ettha nirujjhamānā nirujjhati. Phoṭṭhabbataṇhā loke piyarūpaṃ sātarūpaṃ, etthesā taṇhā pahīyamānā pahīyati, ettha nirujjhamānā nirujjhati. Dhammataṇhā loke piyarūpaṃ sātarūpaṃ, etthesā taṇhā pahīyamānā pahīyati, ettha nirujjhamānā nirujjhati.

Rūpavitakko loke piyarūpaṃ sātarūpaṃ, etthesā taṇhā pahīyamānā pahīyati, ettha nirujjhamānā nirujjhati. Saddavitakko loke piyarūpaṃ sātarūpaṃ, etthesā taṇhā pahīyamānā pahīyati, ettha nirujjhamānā nirujjhati. Gandhavitakko loke piyarūpaṃ sātarūpaṃ, etthesā taṇhā pahīyamānā pahīyati, ettha nirujjhamānā nirujjhati. Rasavitakko loke piyarūpaṃ sātarūpaṃ, etthesā taṇhā pahīyamānā pahīyati, ettha nirujjhamānā nirujjhati. Phoṭṭhabbavitakko loke piyarūpaṃ sātarūpaṃ, etthesā taṇhā pahīyamānā pahīyati, ettha nirujjhamānā nirujjhati. Dhammavitakko loke piyarūpaṃ sātarūpaṃ, etthesā taṇhā pahīyamānā pahīyati, ettha nirujjhamānā nirujjhati.

The craving after visible objects in the world [of mind and matter] is enticing and pleasurable; there this craving may be eradicated and extinguished. The craving after sounds … is enticing and pleasurable; there this craving may be eradicated and extinguished. The craving after smells … is enticing and pleasurable; there this craving may be eradicated and extinguished. The craving after tastes … is enticing and pleasurable; there this craving may be eradicated and extinguished. The craving after touch … is enticing and pleasurable; there this craving may be eradicated and extinguished. The craving after mental contents in the world [of mind and matter] is enticing and pleasurable; there this craving may be eradicated and extinguished.

The thought conception of visible objects in the world [of mind and matter] is enticing and pleasurable; there this craving may be eradicated and extinguished. The thought conception of sounds … is enticing and pleasurable; there this craving may be eradicated and extinguished. The thought conception of smells … is enticing and pleasurable; there this craving may be eradicated and extinguished. The thought conception of tastes … is enticing and pleasurable; there this craving may be eradicated and extinguished. The thought conception of touch … is enticing and pleasurable; there this craving may be eradicated and extinguished. The thought conception of mental contents in the world [of mind and matter] is enticing and pleasurable; there this craving may be eradicated and extinguished.

Rūpavicāro loke piyarūpaṃ sātarūpaṃ, etthesā taṇhā pahīyamānā pahīyati, ettha nirujjhamānā nirujjhati. Saddavicāro loke piyarūpaṃ sātarūpaṃ, etthesā taṇhā pahīyamānā pahīyati, ettha nirujjhamānā nirujjhati. Gandhavicāro loke piyarūpaṃ sātarūpaṃ, etthesā taṇhā pahīyamānā pahīyati, ettha nirujjhamānā nirujjhati. Rasavicāro loke piyarūpaṃ sātarūpaṃ, etthesā taṇhā pahīyamānā pahīyati, ettha nirujjhamānā nirujjhati. Phoṭṭhabbavicāro loke piyarūpaṃ sātarūpaṃ, etthesā taṇhā pahīyamānā pahīyati, ettha nirujjhamānā nirujjhati. Dhammavicāro loke piyarūpaṃ sātarūpaṃ, etthesā taṇhā pahīyamānā pahīyati, ettha nirujjhamānā nirujjhati.

Idaṃ vuccati, bhikkhave, dukkhanirodhaṃ ariyasaccaṃ.

Maggasaccaniddeso

Katamaṃ ca, bhikkhave, dukkhanirodhagāminī paṭipadā ariyasaccaṃ? Ayameva ariyo aṭṭhaṅgiko maggo, seyyathidaṃ, sammādiṭṭhi, sammāsaṅkappo, sammāvācā, sammākammanto, sammā-ājīvo, sammāvāyāmo, sammāsati, sammāsamādhi.

Katamā ca, bhikkhave, sammādiṭṭhi? Yaṃ kho, bhikkhave, dukkhe ñāṇaṃ, dukkhasamudaye ñāṇaṃ, dukkhanirodhe ñāṇaṃ, dukkhanirodhagāminiyā paṭipadāya ñāṇaṃ. Ayaṃ vuccati, bhikkhave, sammādiṭṭhi.

Katamo ca, bhikkhave, sammāsaṅkappo? Nekkhamma-saṅkappo, abyāpādasaṅkappo, avihiṃsā-saṅkappo. Ayaṃ vuccati, bhikkhave, sammāsaṅkappo.

The rolling in thoughts of visible objects in the world [of mind and matter] is enticing and pleasurable; there this craving may be eradicated and extinguished. The rolling in thoughts of sounds... is enticing and pleasurable; there this craving may be eradicated and extinguished. The rolling in thoughts of smells... is enticing and pleasurable; there this craving may be eradicated and extinguished. The rolling in thoughts of tastes... is enticing and pleasurable; there this craving may be eradicated and extinguished. The rolling in thoughts of touch... is enticing and pleasurable; there this craving may be eradicated and extinguished. The rolling in thoughts of mental contents in the world [of mind and matter] is enticing and pleasurable; there this craving may be eradicated and extinguished.

This, monks, is the Noble Truth of the Cessation of Suffering.

Exposition of the Truth of the Path

And what, monks, is the Noble Truth of the Path Leading to the Cessation of Suffering? It is this, the Noble Eightfold Path, namely: right understanding, right thought, right speech, right action, right livelihood, right effort, right awareness and right concentration.

And what, monks, is Right Understanding? It is this, monks: the knowledge of suffering, the knowledge of the arising of suffering, the knowledge of the cessation of suffering, the knowledge of the path leading to the cessation of suffering. This, monks, is called Right Understanding.

And what, monks, is Right Thought? Thoughts of renunciation, thoughts that are free from aversion and thoughts that are free from violence. This, monks, is called Right Thought.

Katamā ca, bhikkhave, sammāvācā? Musāvādā veramaṇī, pisuṇāya vācāya veramaṇī, pharusāya vācāya veramaṇī, samphappalāpā veramaṇī. Ayaṃ vuccati, bhikkhave, sammāvācā.

Katamo ca, bhikkhave, sammākammanto? Pāṇātipātā veramaṇī, adinnādānā veramaṇī, kāmesumicchācārā veramaṇī. Ayaṃ vuccati, bhikkhave, sammākammanto.

Katamo ca, bhikkhave, sammā-ājīvo? Idha, bhikkhave, ariyasāvako micchā-ājīvaṃ pahāya sammā-ājīvena jīvitaṃ kappeti. Ayaṃ vuccati, bhikkhave, sammā-ājīvo.

Katamo ca, bhikkhave, sammāvāyāmo? Idha, bhikkhave, bhikkhu anuppannānaṃ pāpakānaṃ akusalānaṃ dhammānaṃ anuppādāya chandaṃ janeti vāyamati vīriyaṃ ārabhati cittaṃ paggaṇhāti padahati; uppannānaṃ pāpakānaṃ akusalānaṃ dhammānaṃ pahānāya chandaṃ janeti vāyamati vīriyaṃ ārabhati cittaṃ paggaṇhāti padahati; anuppannānaṃ kusalānaṃ dhammānaṃ uppādāya chandaṃ janeti vāyamati vīriyaṃ ārabhati cittaṃ paggaṇhāti padahati; uppannānaṃ kusalānaṃ dhammānaṃ ṭhitiyā asammosāya bhiyyobhāvāya vepullāya bhāvanāya pāripūriyā chandaṃ janeti vāyamati vīriyaṃ ārabhati cittaṃ paggaṇhāti padahati. Ayaṃ vuccati, bhikkhave, sammāvāyāmo.

And what, monks, is Right Speech? Abstaining from lying, abstaining from slander and backbiting, abstaining from harsh words and abstaining from frivolous talk. This, monks, is called Right Speech.

And what, monks, is Right Action? Abstaining from killing, abstaining from taking what has not been given and abstaining from sexual misconduct. This, monks, is called Right Action.

And what, monks, is Right Livelihood? Here, monks, a noble disciple having given up wrong ways of livelihood earns his livelihood by right means. This, monks, is called Right Livelihood.

And what, monks, is Right Effort? Here, monks, a monk generates the will to prevent the arising of unarisen evil unwholesome mental states; he makes strong effort, stirs up his energy, applies his mind to it and strives. To eradicate those evil unwholesome mental states that have arisen in him, he generates the will, makes strong effort, stirs up his energy, applies his mind to it and strives. To develop wholesome mental states that have not yet arisen in him, he generates will, makes strong effort, stirs up his energy, applies his mind to it and strives. To maintain wholesome mental states that have arisen in him, not to let them fade away, to multiply them and bring them to full maturity and to full development, he generates will, makes strong effort, stirs up his energy, applies his mind to it and strives. This, monks, is called Right Effort.

Katamā ca, bhikkhave, sammāsati? Idha, bhikkhave, bhikkhu kāye kāyānupassī viharati ātāpī sampajāno satimā, vineyya loke abhijjhādomanassaṃ, vedanāsu vedanānupassī viharati ātāpī sampajāno satimā, vineyya loke abhijjhādomanassaṃ, citte cittānupassī viharati ātāpī sampajāno satimā, vineyya loke abhijjhādomanassaṃ, dhammesu dhammānupassī viharati ātāpī sampajāno satimā, vineyya loke abhijjhādomanassaṃ. Ayaṃ vuccati, bhikkhave, sammāsati.

Katamo ca, bhikkhave, sammāsamādhi? Idha, bhikkhave, bhikkhu vivicceva kāmehi vivicca akusalehi dhammehi savitakkaṃ savicāraṃ[27] vivekajaṃ pītisukhaṃ paṭhamaṃ jhānaṃ upasampajja viharati, vitakkavicārānaṃ vūpasamā ajjhattaṃ sampasādanaṃ cetaso ekodibhāvaṃ avitakkaṃ avicāraṃ samādhijaṃ pītisukhaṃ dutiyaṃ jhānaṃ upasampajja viharati, pītiyā ca virāgā upekkhako ca viharati sato ca sampajāno sukhaṃ ca kāyena paṭisaṃvedeti yaṃ taṃ ariyā ācikkhanti: 'upekkhako satimā sukhavihārī' ti tatiyaṃ jhānaṃ upasampajja viharati, sukhassa ca pahānā dukkhassa ca pahānā pubbeva somanassadomanassānaṃ atthaṅgamā adukkhamasukhaṃ upekkhāsatipārisuddhiṃ catutthaṃ jhānaṃ upasampajja viharati. Ayaṃ vuccati, bhikkhave, sammāsamādhi.

And what, monks, is Right Awareness? Here, monks, a monk dwells ardent with awareness and constant thorough understanding of impermanence, observing body in body, having removed craving and aversion towards the world [of mind and matter]; he dwells ardent with awareness and constant thorough understanding of impermanence, observing sensations in sensations, having removed craving and aversion towards the world [of mind and matter]; he dwells ardent with awareness and constant thorough understanding of impermanence, observing mind in mind, having removed craving and aversion towards the world [of mind and matter]; he dwells ardent with awareness and constant thorough understanding of impermanence, observing mental contents in mental contents, having removed craving and aversion towards the world [of mind and matter]. This, monks, is called Right Awareness.

And what monks is right concentration? Here monks, a monk, detached from craving, detached from unwholesome mental states, enters into the first absorption, born of detachment, accompanied by initial and sustained application of the mind[27] and filled with rapture and bliss and he dwells therein. With the subsiding of initial and sustained application of the mind and gaining inner tranquility and oneness of mind he enters into the second absorption, born of concentration, free from initial and sustained application of the mind, filled with rapture and bliss and he dwells therein. After the fading away of rapture he dwells in equanimity, aware with constant thorough understanding of impermanence, and he experiences in his body the bliss of which the noble ones say: "That bliss is experienced by one with equanimity and awareness." Thus he enters the third absorption and dwells therein. After the eradication of pleasure and pain and with joy and grief having previously passed away, he enters into a state beyond pleasure and pain, the fourth absorption, that is totally purified by equanimity and awareness and he dwells therein. This, monks, is called Right Concentration.

Idaṃ vuccati, bhikkhave, dukkhanirodhagāminī paṭipadā ariyasaccaṃ.

Iti ajjhattaṃ vā dhammesu dhammānupassī viharati, bahiddhā vā dhammesu dhammānupassī viharati, ajjhattabahiddhā vā dhammesu dhammānupassī viharati, samudayadhammānupassī vā dhammesu viharati, vayadhammānupassī vā dhammesu viharati, samudayavaya-dhammānupassī vā dhammesu viharati, 'atthi dhammā' ti vā panassa sati paccupaṭṭhitā hoti. Yāvadeva ñāṇamattāya paṭissatimattāya anissito ca viharati, na ca kiñci loke upādiyati. Evaṃ pi kho, bhikkhave, bhikkhu dhammesu dhammānupassī viharati catūsu ariyasaccesu.

6. Satipaṭṭhānabhāvanānisaṃso

Yo hi koci, bhikkhave, ime cattāro satipaṭṭhāne evaṃ[28] bhāveyya sattavassāni, tassa dvinnaṃ phalānaṃ aññataraṃ phalaṃ pāṭikaṅkhaṃ: diṭṭheva dhamme aññā,[29] sati vā upādisese anāgāmitā.[30]

Tiṭṭhantu, bhikkhave, sattavassāni. Yo hi koci, bhikkhave, ime cattāro satipaṭṭhāne evaṃ bhāveyya cha vassāni, tassa dvinnaṃ phalānaṃ aññataraṃ phalaṃ pāṭikaṅkhaṃ: diṭṭheva dhamme aññā, sati vā upādisese anāgāmitā.

Tiṭṭhantu, bhikkhave, cha vassāni...pe.

Tiṭṭhantu, bhikkhave, pañca vassāni...pe.

Tiṭṭhantu, bhikkhave, cattāri vassāni...pe.

Tiṭṭhantu, bhikkhave, tīṇi vassāni...pe.

Tiṭṭhantu, bhikkhave, dve vassāni...pe.

This, monks, is the Noble Truth of the Path leading to the Cessation of Suffering.

Thus he dwells observing mental contents in mental contents internally, or he dwells observing mental contents in mental contents externally, or he dwells observing mental contents in mental contents both internally and externally. Thus he dwells observing the phenomenon of arising in the mental contents, thus he dwells observing the phenomenon of passing away in the mental contents, thus he dwells observing the phenomenon of arising and passing away in the mental contents. Now his awareness is established: "These are mental contents!" Thus he develops his awareness to such an extent that there is mere understanding along with mere awareness. In this way he dwells detached, without clinging towards anything in the world [of mind and matter]. This is how, monks, a monk dwells observing mental contents in mental contents as regards the Four Noble Truths.

6. The Results of the Establishing of Awareness

Indeed, monks, whoever practises this fourfold establishing of awareness in this manner[28] for seven years, he may expect one of two results: in this very life highest wisdom[29] or, if a substratum of aggregates remains, the stage of non-returner.[30]

Let alone seven years, monks. Should any person practise this fourfold establishing of awareness in this manner for six years, one of two results may be expected in him: in this very life highest wisdom or, if a substratum of aggregates remains, the stage of non-returner.

Let alone six years, monks...

Let alone five years, monks...

Let alone four years, monks...

Let alone three years, monks...

Let alone two years, monks...

Tiṭṭhatu, bhikkhave, ekaṃ vassaṃ. Yo hi koci, bhikkhave, ime cattāro satipaṭṭhāne evaṃ bhāveyya sattamāsāni, tassa dvinnaṃ phalānaṃ aññataraṃ phalaṃ pāṭikaṅkhaṃ: diṭṭheva dhamme aññā, sati vā upādisese anāgāmitā.

Tiṭṭhantu, bhikkhave, satta māsāni...pe.

Tiṭṭhantu, bhikkhave, cha māsāni...pe.

Tiṭṭhantu, bhikkhave, pañca māsāni...pe.

Tiṭṭhantu, bhikkhave, cattāri māsāni...pe.

Tiṭṭhantu, bhikkhave, tīṇi māsāni...pe.

Tiṭṭhantu, bhikkhave, dve māsāni...pe.

Tiṭṭhatu, bhikkhave, ekaṃ māsaṃ...pe.

Tiṭṭhatu, bhikkhave, aḍḍhamāsaṃ...pe.

Tiṭṭhatu, bhikkhave, aḍḍhamāso. Yo hi koci, bhikkhave, ime cattāro satipaṭṭhāne evaṃ bhāveyya sattāhaṃ, tassa dvinnaṃ phalānaṃ aññataraṃ phalaṃ pāṭikaṅkhaṃ: diṭṭheva dhamme aññā, sati vā upādisese anāgāmitā.

'Ekāyano ayaṃ, bhikkhave, maggo sattānaṃ visuddhiyā, sokaparidevānaṃ samatikkamāya, dukkhadomanassānaṃ atthaṅgamāya, ñāyassa adhigamāya, nibbānassa sacchikiriyāya yadidaṃ cattāro satipaṭṭhānā' ti. Iti yaṃ taṃ vuttaṃ, idametaṃ paṭicca vuttaṃ ti.

Idamavoca bhagavā. Attamanā te bhikkhū bhagavato bhāsitaṃ abhinanduṃ ti.

Mahāsatipaṭṭhāna-suttaṃ niṭṭhitaṃ.

Let alone one year, monks. Should any person practise this fourfold establishing of awareness in this manner for seven months, one of two results may be expected in him: in this very life highest wisdom or, if a substratum of aggregates remains, the stage of non-returner.

Let alone seven months, monks...

Let alone six months, monks...

Let alone five months, monks...

Let alone four months, monks...

Let alone three months, monks...

Let alone two months, monks...

Let alone one month, monks...

Let alone half a month, monks...

Let alone half a month, monks. Should any person practise this fourfold establishing of awareness in this manner for seven days, one of two results may be expected in him: in this very life highest wisdom or, if a substratum of aggregates remains, the stage of non-returner.

It is for this reason that it was said: "This is the one and only way, monks, for the purification of beings, for the overcoming of sorrow and lamentation, for the extinguishing of suffering and grief, for walking on the path of truth, for the realisation of *nibbāna:* that is to say, the fourfold establishing of awareness."

Thus the Enlightened One spoke. Glad in heart, the monks welcomed the words of the Enlightened One.

The End of the Mahāsatipaṭṭhāna Sutta

Notes

N.B. For clarity, the footnoted passage will be indicated in the notes by Pāli in italics followed immediately by the English translation in square brackets, e.g. *sati* [awareness]. Other Pāli words used in the notes will be followed by their equivalent terms in parentheses where appropriate, e.g. *anicca* (impermanence).

1. The word *bhikkhū* [monks] was used to address all the people who listened to the discourses given by the Buddha. Thus every meditator, everyone who is walking on the path of Dhamma, though not literally a *bhikkhu,* can benefit by following the instructions given here.
2. *Satipaṭṭhāna* [establishing of awareness] *Sati* means "awareness." *Satipaṭṭhāna* implies that the meditator has to work diligently and constantly to become firmly established in awareness or mindfulness. Therefore we have used "the establishing of awareness," to convey the sense that one actively strives to maintain continuous awareness of mind and body at the level of sensations, as will become clear from the rest of the discourse.

   There are certain passages in the Buddha's discourses where *sati* has the meaning of "memory." (*Dīgha-nikāya:* VRI.I.411; II.374; PTS.I.180; II.292). This is especially true when he refers to the special ability of remembering past lives which is developed by means of the practice of the *jhānas* (deep absorption concentration). But in the context of *Satipaṭṭhāna,* the practice of Vipassana, leading not to the *jhānas* but to purification of mind, *sati* can only be understood to mean awareness of the present moment rather than a memory of the past (or a dream of the future).
3. The Buddha always included the term *sampajañña* [constant thorough understanding of impermanence] or *sampajāno* (the adjective form of *sampajañña*) whenever he was asked to explain *sati* (awareness). (See, for example, the definition of *sammāsati* in the Chapter on the Four Noble Truths: Truth of the Path.) As a result

of the frequent association of these words, *sampajañña* has often been defined as nearly synonymous with *sati*—as "full awareness," or "clear comprehension"—or as an exhortation to remain mindful. Another translation of *sampajañña*, which is closer to the full meaning is "thorough understanding."

In the *Sutta Piṭaka* the Buddha gave two explanations of the term. In the *Saṃyutta-nikāya* (VRI.III.401; PTS.V.180-1) he defines it as follows:

> *Kathañca, bhikkhave, bhikkhu sampajāno hoti? Idha bhikkhave, bhikkhuno viditā vedanā uppajjanti, viditā upaṭṭhahanti, viditā abbhatthaṃ gacchanti; viditā saññā uppajjanti, viditā upaṭṭhahanti, viditā abbhatthaṃ gacchanti; viditā vitakkā uppajjanti, viditā upaṭṭhahanti, viditā abbhatthaṃ gacchanti. Evaṃ kho, bhikkhave, bhikkhu sampajāno hoti.*
>
> And how, monks, does a monk understand thoroughly? Here, monks, a monk experiences sensations arising in him, experiences their persisting, and experiences their vanishing; he experiences perceptions arising in him, experiences their persisting, and experiences their vanishing; he experiences each initial application of the mind [on an object] arising in him, experiences its persisting, and experiences its vanishing. This, monks, is how a monk understands thoroughly.

In the above statement it is clear that one is *sampajāno* only when one understands the characteristic of impermanence (arising, persisting and vanishing). This understanding must be based on sensation *(viditā vedanā)*. If the characteristic of impermanence is not experienced at the level of *vedanā*, then one's understanding is merely an intellectualization, since it is only through sensation that direct experience occurs. The statement further indicates that *sampajañña* lies in the experience of the impermanence of *saññā* and *vitakkā*. Here we should note that impermanence understood at the level of *vedanā* actually covers all three cases since according to the Buddha's teaching in the *Mūlaka Sutta* of the *Aṅguttara-nikāya* (VRI.III. *Dasakanipāta*, 58; PTS.V.107):

Vedanā-samosaraṇā sabbe dhammā.

Everything that arises in the mind flows together with sensations.

The second explanation of *sampajañña* given by the Buddha emphasizes that it must be continuous. In several places he repeats the words of the *Sampajānapabbaṃ* of *Mahāsatipaṭṭhāna Sutta*, as in this passage from the *Mahāparinibbāna Sutta* (*Dīgha-nikāya:* VRI.II.160; PTS.II.95):

> *Kathañca, bhikkhave, bhikkhu sampajāno hoti? Idha bhikkhave, bhikkhu abhikkante paṭikkante sampajānakārī hoti, ālokite vilokite sampajānakārī hoti, samiñjite pasārite sampajānakārī hoti, saṅghāṭipattacīvaradhāraṇe sampajānakārī hoti, asite pīte khāyite sāyite sampajānakārī hoti, uccārapassāvakamme sampajānakārī hoti, gate ṭhite nisinne sutte jāgarite bhāsite tuṇhībhāve sampajānakārī hoti.*
>
> And how, monks, does a monk understand thoroughly? Here, monks, a monk, while going forward or backward, he does so with constant thorough understanding of impermanence; whether he is looking straight ahead or looking sideways, he does so with constant thorough understanding of impermanence; while he is bending or stretching, he does so with constant thorough understanding of impermanence; whether wearing his robes or carrying his bowl, he does so with constant thorough understanding of impermanence; whether he is eating, drinking, chewing or savouring, he does so with constant thorough understanding of impermanence; while attending to the calls of nature, he does so with constant thorough understanding of impermanence; whether he is walking, standing, sitting, sleeping or waking, speaking or in silence, he does so with constant thorough understanding of impermanence.

With proper understanding of the teaching of the Buddha, it becomes clear that if this continuous *sampajañña* consists only of the thorough understanding of the external processes of walking, eating, and other activities of the body, then what is being practised is merely *sati*. If, however, the constant thorough understanding includes the characteristic of the arising and passing away of *vedanā* while the meditator is performing these activities, then *sampajāno satimā* is being practised, *paññā* (wisdom) is being developed.

The Buddha describes this more specifically in this passage from the *Aṅguttara-nikāya* (VRI.I, *Catukkanipāta,* 12; PTS.II.15) in words reminiscent of *Sampajānapabbaṃ:*

Yataṃ care yataṃ tiṭṭhe, yataṃ acche yataṃ saye
yataṃ samiñjaye bhikkhu, yatamenaṃ pasāraye
uddhaṃ tiriyaṃ apācīnaṃ, yāvatā jagato gati,
samavekkhitā ca dhammānaṃ, khandhānaṃ udayabbayaṃ.

Whether the monk walks or stands or sits or lies,
whether he bends or stretches, above, across, backwards,
whatever his course in the world,
he observes the arising and passing away of the aggregates.

The Buddha clearly emphasized the thorough understanding of *anicca* (impermanence) in all bodily and mental activities. Therefore, since the proper understanding of this technical term, *sampajañña,* is so critical for an understanding of this *sutta,* we have translated it as "the constant thorough understanding of impermanence," even though this definition is less concise than the traditional "thorough understanding."

4. In this introductory paragraph the Buddha repeats a basic verbal formula reminding us that we must continuously observe "body in body," or "sensations in sensations," or "mind in mind," or "mental contents in mental contents." Though these verbal constructs may seem unusual, they refer to the fact that this observation has to be directly experiential rather than dealing only with thought, imagination or contemplation of the object.

The Buddha emphasizes this point in the *Ānāpānasati Sutta* (*Majjhima-nikāya* III: VRI. 149; PTS 83-4), where he describes the progressive stages of the practice of *ānāpāna* meditation. In the section where he explains how the four *satipaṭṭhānā* are brought to perfection by *ānāpāna* he says:

...kāyesu kāyaññatarāhaṃ, bhikkhave, evaṃ vadāmi yadidaṃ assāsapassāsā. Tasmātiha, bhikkhave, kāye kāyānupassī tasmiṃ

> *samaye bhikkhu viharati ātāpī sampajāno satimā vineyya loke abhijjhādomanassaṃ.*
>
> ...Monks, when I say, 'inhalation-exhalation,' it is like another body in the body. Observing body in body in this way, monks, at that time a monk dwells ardent with awareness and constant thorough understanding of impermanence, having removed craving and aversion towards this world [of mind and matter].

This indicates that practising *ānāpāna* meditation leads directly to experiencing the body, which means feeling sensations in the body. The sensations may be related to the breath, the oxygen flowing in the blood, etc. but those details are not important. The body-in-body experience is not imagined or contemplated but felt throughout the body. More specifically, he continues:

> *...vedanāsu vedanāññatarāhaṃ, bhikkhave, evaṃ vadāmi yadidaṃ assāsapassāsānaṃ sādhukaṃ manasikāraṃ. Tasmātiha, bhikkhave, vedanāsu vedanānupassī tasmiṃ samaye bhikkhu viharati ātāpī sampajāno satimā vineyya loke abhijjhādomanassaṃ.*
>
> ...monks, when I say, 'by proper attention to inhalation-exhalation,' it is like other sensations in the sensations. Observing sensations in sensations in this way, monks, at that time a monk dwells ardent with awareness and constant thorough understanding of impermanence, having removed craving and aversion towards this world [of mind and matter].

By equating the observation of the breath with experiencing sensations the Buddha is pointing to the critical importance of the body and the sensations in proper practice of meditation. It is the awareness of these sensations by direct experience throughout the body, while maintaining equanimity with the understanding of impermanence, that perfects the four *satipaṭṭhānas.*

It is instructive that in *Ānāpānasati Sutta* he describes the experience of body-in-body and sensations-in-sensations as one observes the breath but when he turns to the observation of mind he does not continue with the same verbal formula. Instead, he again directs our attention to the importance of *sampajañña*:

> *...citte cittānupassī, bhikkhave, tasmiṃ samaye bhikkhu viharati ātāpī sampajāno satimā vineyya loke abhijjhādomanassaṃ. Nāhaṃ, bhikkhave, muṭṭhassatissa asampajānassa ānāpānassatiṃ vadāmi.*
>
> ...observing mind in mind, monks, at that time a monk dwells ardent with awareness and constant thorough understanding of impermanence, having removed craving and aversion towards this world [of mind and matter]. I say, monks, one who is inattentive, who is not constantly aware of impermanence, he is not one doing *ānāpāna.*

Beginning with *ānāpāna* as a starting point the practice described has led directly to Vipassana, i.e., to the practice of the four *satipaṭṭhānas.* And here we see how emphatically the Buddha states that, even while observing the mind, one is not practising properly unless there is awareness of impermanence with the direct experience of the sensations.

5. *Pajānāti* [understands properly] means, "to understand, to know deeply or intently with wisdom." It is the result of the intensification of the verb *jānāti* (he or she knows) by the addition of the prefix *pa-*, from *paññā* (wisdom).

6. *Iti ajjhattaṃ...kāye kāyānupassī viharati.* [Thus he dwells...dwells observing body in body.] This paragraph is repeated twenty-one times throughout the *Mahāsatipaṭṭhāna Sutta,* with variations according to which section of the four *satipaṭṭhānas* one has reached: body, sensations, mind or mental contents.

   In this key paragraph the Buddha describes the common steps in Vipassana that all meditators must pass through no matter what section of the *sutta* one begins with. In each repetition, this paragraph focuses our attention on the essential fact that, no matter if one is observing body, sensations, mind or mental contents, one must understand the fundamental characteristic of arising and passing away. This understanding of impermanence then leads directly to the total detachment from the world of mind and matter which takes us to *nibbāna* (liberation).

7. *Bahiddhā* [externally] is sometimes translated as "outer things" or "observing another's body." In the following section, on the observation of sensations, it has sometimes been taken to mean "feeling the sensations of others." While such an experience is not impossible, it would be practised only at a very high stage of development. According to the *sutta*, the meditator is asked to sit alone somewhere in a forest, under a tree or in an empty room, and start practising. In such a situation observing others would be meaningless, and the sensations of someone or something else would be of no use. For a meditator, therefore, "externally," meaning the surface of the body, is the most practical definition of *bahiddhā.*

   See also note no. 19.

8. The Pāli *atthi kāyo* [this is body] indicates that the meditator at this stage clearly understands experientially, at the level of sensations, "body" in its true nature: its characteristic of arising and passing away. Therefore the meditator neither makes any identification of "body" as male or female, young or old, beautiful or ugly, etc., nor has any attachment towards "I," "me," or "mine."

   In the other three sections of the *sutta*, the sensations, mind and mental contents are each identified similarly in their corresponding paragraphs: "This is sensation," "This is mind," "These are mental contents," to indicate the lack of identification of the meditator with the object, and his or her understanding of the object in its true characteristic of *anicca* (impermanence).

9. *Yāvadeva ñāṇamattāya paṭissatimattāya* [Thus he develops his awareness to such an extent that there is mere understanding along with mere awareness.] The mind of the meditator at this stage is absorbed in the wisdom of *anicca* (the arising and passing away of sensations), with no identification beyond this awareness. With the base of this awareness he develops understanding with his own experience. This is *paññā* (wisdom). With his awareness thus established in *anicca*, there is no attraction to the world of mind and matter.

10. This includes the changing of position as well as the four basic postures of the body. Whatever one does, an ardent meditator is always aware with wisdom: *yathā yathā vā...tathā tathā naṃ pajānāti* (whatever he does...that he understands properly).

11. *Sampajānakārī hoti* [does so with constant thorough understanding of impermanence] literally means: "He is doing (all the time) *sampajañña.*" It is helpful to follow the progression of the Buddha's words in Pāli: he uses *"jānāti"* (he knows), *"pajānāti"* (understands properly—intently or deeply with wisdom), and *"sampajānāti"* (he constantly and thoroughly understands the impermanent nature of his experience). Each word indicates a progressive step, that the meditator takes by following the instructions given in the *sutta.* Thus he proceeds from simple experience, to understanding based on direct experience, up to thorough and constant understanding of the impermanence, at the level of sensations, of each and every experience.

12. *Sāmisa* [with attachment] literally means: *sa-āmisa* (with-flesh); *nirāmisa* [without attachment]: means *nir-āmisa* (without-flesh). They can also be rendered as: "impure" and "pure," "material" and "immaterial" or, "sensual" and "nonsensual." A common interpretation is that a sensation which is *sāmisa* is related to the world of sensual pleasures and a *nirāmisa* sensation is a sensation related to the higher meditational realms.

    In this context, related to the observation of sensations without any reaction of craving or aversion by the meditator, we have used "with attachment" and "without attachment." These terms seem clearest insofar as they relate to the practice.

13. See note no. 7.

14. *Citta* [mind], in this context, is correctly translated as "mind." The meditator experiences different states of mind and observes them in an objective and detached manner. It might be misleading to translate *citta* here as "thought."

    Citte cittānupassī [mind in mind] refers to the experiential nature of the observation required (see note no. 4).

15. *Saṅkhittaṃ* [collected] and *vikkhittaṃ* [scattered] correspond to mental states either scattered because of the *pañcā nīvaraṇā*, the "five hindrances," or collected when the hindrances are not manifesting their respective effects. (See the following Section 5A, The Hindrances.)
16. *Mahaggataṃ cittaṃ* [expanded mind] means literally: "mind having become great;" i.e., by the practice and development of the *jhānas* (the practice of absorption *samādhi*). It refers to a mind expanded by the practice of these deep *samādhis,* rather than the stage transcending mind and matter. *Amahaggataṃ cittaṃ* [unexpanded mind] thus means a mind not having become expanded in this way.
17. *Sa-uttaraṃ* [surpassable] means: "having something higher than that" or "not superior." This type of mind is still connected with the mundane field. *Anuttaraṃ* [unsurpassable], correspondingly, is a mind that has reached a very high stage of meditation, where nothing is superior. Therefore "surpassable" and "unsurpassable," though not very precise, seem to be the nearest translations.
18. *Samāhitaṃ* [concentrated] and *asamāhitaṃ* [unconcentrated] are related to the type of *samādhi* (concentration) that one has gained; states of concentration that are called: *upacāra* (neighbourhood concentration, i.e. approaching a level of absorption) and *appanā samādhi* (absorption, or attainment, concentration). *Asamāhitaṃ cittaṃ* therefore describes a mental state without that depth of concentration.
19. *Iti ajjhattaṃ...bahiddhā...ajjhattabahiddhā vā citte cittānupassī viharati* [Thus he dwells observing mind in mind internally... externally...both internally and externally]. Applied to the mind (and in the next section, the mental contents) this sentence has sometimes been interpreted to mean that the meditator observes his own mind (internally) and the mind of others (externally). This can be done only by a very highly developed meditator, therefore it is not a practical instruction for most people.

In this section the meditator is asked to experience directly the mind in mind *(citte cittānupassī).* This can be done only by observing whatever arises in the mind. As the body was experienced by means of what arises on the body (i.e., sensation); the mind is experienced only when something arises in the mind (i.e., the mental contents). When the mind is observing the internal objects—its own internal mental states—it is observing the mind in mind internally.

To observe the mind and mental contents externally means to observe experientially that any object which comes in contact with the mind-body through any of the six sense doors (that is, an external stimulus) causes an internal reaction. Any sight, sound, taste, smell, touch or thought results in a sensation and the mind feels it. Of course, internal mental states and sensation resulting from contact with external objects will all mix and flow together.

Therefore, again, we see the importance of the Buddha's statement:

> *Vedanā-samosaraṇā sabbe dhammā.*
>
> Everything that arises in the mind flows together with sensations. (*Mūlaka Sutta: Aṅguttara-nikāya* VRI.III, *Dasakanipāta*, 58; PTS.V.107)

Whether the object is internal or external, if the mind remains within the body observing the sensations, then it is directly experiencing the mind and mental contents in a tangible way that easily allows the meditator to experience the impermanent nature of the entire mind-matter phenomenon.

20. *Pañca upādānakkhandhā* [the five aggregates of clinging] consist of: *rūpakkhandha* (the material aggregate) connected with *kāya* (body) and the four *nāmakkhandhā* (aggregates of mind), which are:

viññāṇakkhandha (the aggregate of consciousness);
saññākkhandha (the aggregate of perception);
vedanākkhandha (the aggregate of feeling body sensations);
saṅkhārakkhandha (the aggregate of reaction).

The *pañca upādānakkhandhā* are aggregates of clinging, or attachment, in two ways. They are the basic objects to which we cling because of our illusion that the five together make up "I," "me." In addition, the continual arising of the aggregates—with the attendant suffering that goes with the cycle of becoming—is due to the clinging toward this illusory "I." Aggregates and clinging always go together, except in the case of an *arahant,* who has *pañca khandhā,* the five aggregates, but no clinging towards them; no *upādāna* (attachment or clinging) is possible for such a person.

21. Here *dhamma* has to be understood as the law of nature, the nature of the law in its totality. At a superficial level *dhammavicaya* [investigation of Dhamma] can be understood to mean intellectual investigation of the law. But to become a factor of enlightenment *dhammavicaya* must become an experiential investigation—direct experience of the phenomenon of arising and passing away at the level of sensations.
22. *Pīti* [rapture] is difficult to translate into English. It is often translated as: "joy," "delight," "bliss" or "thrill." Each of these words conveys at least partially the meaning of mental and physical pleasantness. For *pīti* to become a factor of enlightenment it must be experienced in its true nature as ephemeral, arising and passing away. Only then can the meditator avoid the danger of becoming attached to the pleasantness of this stage.
23. As with the previous factor of enlightenment, *passaddhi* [tranquillity], becomes a factor of enlightenment only when it is experienced as impermanent, *anicca*—arising and passing away. The danger for the meditator here is that this stage of deep tranquillity might be mistaken for the final goal of *nibbāna.* This deep illusion *(moha)* is removed by the experience of *anicca* as one experiences this tranquillity.
24. In the texts *byādhi* [sickness] is sometimes included, sometimes omitted.
25. Here it is very clear that the word *dukkha* [pain] is related to the body, and *domanassa* [grief] to the mind. Correspondingly, *sukha*

(bodily pleasure) is related to the body, *somanassa* (mental pleasure) to the mind and *adukkhamasukha* (neither painful nor pleasant) as neutral, to both body and mind.

26. The word *loke* [world] has a wide spectrum of meaning: "universe," "world," "region," "people." In this entire section it is used in connection with everything that one experiences at any of the six senses, and the entire process of the contact between the senses and their respective objects. So in this context *loke* is to be understood as the "world" of the mind-body phenomenon. Therefore the entire "world" can be directly experienced at the level of the sensations in the body that result from any of these interactions.

27. *Vitakko* [thought conception] refers to the initial application of the mind to an object. This is contrasted with *vicāro* [rolling in thoughts] in the next paragraph, which refers to a sustained application of the mind on an object.

    In the later section, dealing with the *jhānas* (see pp. 76, 77), the translation reflects this relationship more directly since the context is one of deep absorption in the object of meditation rather than one where mental impurities are arising.

28. *Evaṃ* [in this manner], as explained throughout the entire *sutta*, is *ātāpī sampajāno satimā* (ardent with awareness of mind and body at the level of sensations and with constant thorough understanding of impermanence). In order to achieve these guaranteed results the continuity should be *sampajaññaṃ na riñcati* ([the meditator] does not lose the constant thorough understanding of impermanence even for a moment).

29. The final stage of liberation of an *arahant*.

30. The stage of an *anāgāmī* [non-returner] is the third and next-to-last stage of liberation.

Courses of Vipassana meditation in the tradition of Sayagyi U Ba Khin as taught by S.N. Goenka are held regularly at more than 150 permanent centers in many countries throughout the world. For information about Vipassana and a schedule of courses, please contact:

www.dhamma.org